Human Resource Management
in Schools and Colleges

WITHDRAWN FROM STOCK

WITHDRAWN FROM STOCK

WITHDRAWN FROM STOCK

Human Resource Management in Schools and Colleges

David Middlewood and Jacky Lumby

EMDU, University of Leicester

P·C·P

Paul Chapman
Publishing Ltd

Barcode No:......*39006045502*

Dewey No:.....*658.3*

Date Input..*29-1-99*

Price....*£27.70*

Copyright © 1998 David Middlewood and Jacky Lumby

First published 1998

All rights reserved. No part of this publication may be reproduced, stored in a retrieval system, transmitted or utilised in any form or by any means, electronic, mechanical, photocopying, recording or otherwise, without permission in writing from the Publishers, except in accordance with the provisions of the Copyright Designs and Patents Act 1988 or under the terms of a licence issued by the Copyright Licensing Agency Ltd, 5 Dryden Street, Covent Garden, London WC2E 9NW, England.

Paul Chapman Publishing Ltd
A SAGE Publications Company
6 Bonhill Street
London EC2A 4PU

SAGE Publications Inc
2455 Teller Road
Thousand Oaks, California 91320

SAGE Publications India Pvt Ltd
32, M-Block Market
Greater Kailash - I
New Delhi 110 048

British Cataloguing in Publication data

A catalogue record for this book is available from the British Library

ISBN 1 95396 432 8
ISBN 1 85396 401 8 (pbk)

Library of Congress catalog card number available

Typeset by Dorwyn Ltd, Rowlands Castle, Hants
Printed and bound in Great Britain by the Cromwell Press, Wiltshire
A B C D E F 3 2 1 0 9 8

Contents

WITHDRAWN FROM STOCK

The authors

David Middlewood and **Jacky Lumby** both work in the Educational Management Development Unit of Leicester University, based in Northampton. They have both written materials for Leicester University's MBA in Educational Management by Distance Learning programme and have both edited volumes and contributed chapters in the series 'Educational Management: Research and Practice', published by Paul Chapman. Together, they have produced *Strategic Management in Schools and Colleges*, published in 1998 in that series.

David Middlewood is Director of School-based programmes in the Unit, and was formerly a secondary school headteacher. He has published on a variety of topics, including *Managing People in Education* (with Tony Bush).

Jacky Lumby is a lecturer in educational management in the Unit, has published on a number of topics, especially on Further Education, and is co-editor (with Nick Foskett) of *Managing External Relations in Schools and Colleges*, published by Paul Chapman.

Acknowledgements

The authors' thanks go to:

John O'Neill who was responsible for some of the original material on which Section A of the book is based.

Felicity Murray for her patience and commitment to ensure the completion of the book through her careful work on the manuscript.

1. Introduction

This book is intended primarily for students taking Advanced courses in Educational Management such as Leicester University's Educational Management Development Unit's MBA in Educational Management. It is therefore written as a teaching text. However, it also offers much to the general reader, especially those working in education, in terms of an opportunity to increase their understanding and knowledge of, and develop their skills in aspects of, educational management.

The specific aims of this book are:

- to equip readers with a body of knowledge that will improve their understanding of human resource management
- to enable readers to reflect on concepts, theories and models of human resource management in education
- to provide a range of analytical frameworks that can be applied by readers to their own working environments
- to provide opportunities for the improvement of their skills in human resource management through site-based research
- to enable readers to contribute to school or college improvement in its management of human resources.

By the end of this book, readers should be able to:

- set their own knowledge of human resource management in a wider context of theory and practice through an awareness of relevant literature in the field
- clarify the linkages between theory, values and strategies in human resource management in their own school or college situation
- critically analyse their own and their institution's current practice in human resource management, using relevant analytical skills
- reflect upon and articulate their own and their institution's values in human resource management
- conduct small-scale research investigations in their own institution in order to generate school or college improvement
- undertake a written assignment on a research-based topic in human resource management.

❏ Activities
In this book we offer a number of activities which should help you to:

- use what you have read to help **examine** your own practice
- constructively **criticise** your and your institution's practice.

These activities enable you to analyse and reflect upon what you have read and relate it to your own management practice, now and in the future. They may also assist you when you are considering a specific topic to investigate for a written assignment.

❏ Linked reading
This text is free-standing and contains ample material for the reader to be able to improve his/her management practice or produce a course assignment or project. However, additional reading is clearly helpful, and for students essential. There are two key books to draw to your attention:

1. *Managing People in Education* (1997) edited by Tony Bush and David Middlewood, published by Paul Chapman. This book examines the implications of educational change in the context of self-

managing schools and colleges for the management of all the people who work in them. Good management practice is articulated on the basis of evidence in educational settings, with the emphasis on applying research findings to improve work practice. We shall refer the reader to precise chapters or sections of the book at regular intervals.

2. *The Principles of Educational Management* (1994) edited by Tony Bush and John West-Burnham, published by Longman. This book covers a wide range of issues in educational management, and some of its chapters relate specifically to human resource issues dealt with in this text.

❏ Structure of this book

Section A proposes a premise on which much of the discussion in the book is based. We describe HRM, both generally and in education, and then point out the balance or tension between the need for managing people as individuals and the need to manage the whole workforce as a unit so that the school or college performs effectively.

In Section B, we examine this balance through a division into those issues which managers must address in thinking of organisation development and 'health' (Chapter 5) and those which are more easily seen from the perspective of the individual (Chapter 6). Of course, the division is artificial, since each person in a school or college has an awareness of both personal and organisational pressures, demands and challenges. However, the division is perhaps helpful in reminding HRM managers that both perspectives, individual and organisational, are critical. An ideal is for the manager to integrate these two perspectives as one.

In Section C, we examine the extent to which this ideal is attainable through effective management by looking at certain areas common to all schools and colleges, such as staff selection and appraisal. Because the principles of people management apply to all who work in schools and colleges, we have not included a chapter specifically on managing associate staff. Most readers of this book studying to Masters level will be teachers or lecturers themselves, many with responsibility for associate staff and other professional colleagues. We believe the principles apply to *all* those who work in schools and colleges. We use the term 'teachers' throughout to mean both teachers in schools and lecturers in colleges, because their prime function *is* teaching. 'Associate staff' means all those working in schools and colleges who are not actually employed as teachers or lecturers, although the distinction between tasks for each is becoming increasingly blurred.

Section A

2. The importance of HRM in education

Introduction: a premise

As you work through this book you will become increasingly aware of our basic argument for the unit as a whole which is that effective human resource management (HRM) is the key to the provision of high quality educational experiences. The term itself, human resource management, may still appear problematic, perhaps even slightly distasteful, in education where concepts of professionalism, professional autonomy and collegial approaches to decision-making militate against the perception of teachers as a resource to be managed, manipulated or directed in pursuit of school or college objectives. We, however, do not see HRM approaches and professionalism as mutually incompatible. Indeed, we base our assertion on an apparently simple premise which we believe would have the support of professional colleagues in schools or colleges:

> Educational organisations depend for their success on the **quality**, **commitment** and **performance** of **people** who work there.

In order to introduce you to the values which underpin **our** understanding of HRM in education we 'unpack' each of our key terms below.

❏ Quality

The quality of staff in educational organisations is an issue of both **specification** and **development**. Informed recruitment and selection procedures are an essential element of specification: what job needs to be done and what sort of person do we need to carry out that job? Quality is, however, about much more than appointing the most suitable candidate.

Drucker (1988) argues that people as a basic resource are unique in the sense that the quality of their performance is dependent on a host of organisational variables. Drucker implies that effective organisations are fully aware of the fact that the management support they provide makes a direct and qualitative difference to the level of performance of individual staff and the contribution they make to the work of the institution.

We imagine that your feelings of increasing confidence and competence in your present post are attributable in no small measure to your personal and professional qualities and skills, but also, in great part, to the support and encouragement which have been provided for you by others within your teaching team, department or institution. Unfortunately, in some instances, the situation may be very different; you, or colleagues or friends, will have experience of working in institutions, or with groups of people, where support and encouragement are not forthcoming; where the prevailing culture is one of 'sink or swim' or learning in the 'school of hard knocks'. Whatever the quality of your own treatment, you will know from your own experience that your professional effectiveness is contingent upon support from others. Effective schools and colleges display a similar awareness and actively manage the levels of support they provide for staff so that the quality of staff contributions increases rather than decreases with time.

❏ Commitment

Wanting to do well, to feel a sense of belonging to a group or team of people working towards the same goals, and being determined to achieve those goals or targets, are natural aspirations for staff in any organisation. Indeed, conscientious classroom teachers constantly attempt to develop those same qualities amongst students with whom they work.

From an HRM perspective, commitment is something that has to be managed, it cannot be assumed. Developing commitment is about:

- **articulating** a clear sense of purpose, so that staff know what they are supposed to be doing and why
- **translating** a sense of purpose into clear and realistic objectives for the institution, groups and individuals
- **providing** opportunities for and **removing** barriers to the achievement of those objectives
- **involving** staff in developing that sense of purpose and identifying targets so that, wherever possible, they feel ownership of their work
- **integrating** staff within the work of the school or college so that they feel their contribution is essential and unique
- **valuing** staff and the qualities, skills and expertise they bring to the organisation.

Effective schools and colleges do not assume that an offer of employment is sufficient to secure commitment but, rather, that gaining commitment involves active encouragement, support and open communication. Various writers (e.g. Beare, Caldwell and Millikan, 1989; Handy, 1994; West-Burnham, 1996) emphasise the active role that needs to be taken by senior managers in organisations in:

- **articulating** organisational values and mission
- **publicising** acceptable performance standards
- **involving** staff in decision-making
- **bringing together** individuals and groups of staff to reinforce common objectives

so that collective commitment to agreed organisational goals can be optimised.

❑ Performance

As we suggest above, quality of performance is not an absolute standard. Performance varies between institutions and individuals according to a host of variables. Performance standards may be defined **for**, **with** or **by** individuals. Performance standards may seek to measure **input**, **process** or **outcome** factors or a combination of the three. They may be **qualitative** or **quantitative** in nature. Often the performance of individuals will depend on contributions from others within the immediate work group.

Traditionally the quality of individual student learning experiences has eluded satisfactory, objective definition. For some institutions ensuring regular attendance and developing basic levels of literacy, numeracy and social skills amongst students constitutes a meaningful and worthwhile set of objectives. For other institutions successful performance may only be measured against a benchmark of acceptable accredited results. For yet others, gaining and sustaining regular eye contact may be the realisation of several years effort on the part of student, teacher, therapist, parent and carer.

Just as the assessment of student attainment is complex, problematic and dependent on context, so it is with the performance of adults employed within educational organisations. The common elements between the two perspectives, however, are:

- the notion of promoting continuous progress and improvement, and
- the provision of support and feedback on performance.

In order to perform at an optimum level adults need:

- **targets** against which they can measure progress
- constructive **feedback** so that impressionistic and potentially subjective observations or assessments of performance are avoided
- **reassurance** that mistakes are an inevitable and necessary part of both learning and higher levels of attainment

- **structured support** so that difficulties can be addressed as they occur and resources provided to support further development
- frequent **recognition** of their achievements and contribution to the success of the school or college.

Observers of effective management practice in non-education sectors (e.g. Handy, 1994; Morgan, 1996) have consistently highlighted the need for organisations to view mistakes positively, as an inevitable by-product of striving for higher standards of performance. This is perhaps a difficult new paradigm for educationalists to understand and adopt in a profession where the majority of practitioners have, historically, operated in classroom isolation, and where direct observation of performance has been the exception rather than the norm. In England and Wales the teaching profession's perceived ambivalence towards the introduction of a variety of mechanisms for increased professional accountability exemplifies the difficulties associated with direct assessment of individual and whole school or college performance (Foreman, 1997, p. 215).

❑ People

It is sometimes assumed that 'people' in educational organisations means **teachers**; not other adults working within the school or college, nor even the students for whose development and learning the institution, in theory, is established. Our understanding of this issue is clear.

1. The management of human resources in education focuses on **all** adults employed within the school or college and, in the case of external agencies and contractors, those who provide a service to the organisation.

2. Although the management of students is not directly our concern in this unit, it is worth noting that many of the **principles** which apply to the effective management of staff apply also to the management of the relationship between teacher and student.

3. The complexities associated with the management of learning in schools and colleges in the 1990s lead us firmly towards the conviction that HRM perspectives need to acknowledge the invaluable contributions made by all categories of staff to the work of the institution. As such we reject the historical iconography of the teacher as sole **provider** of support for student learning, as sole **arbiter** of what takes place within the classroom and as sole **worker** in the preparation, delivery and administration of all activities associated with the provision and assessment of teaching and learning. It is, perhaps, only with the introduction of financial autonomy at school and college level that institutions have begun to fully debate the merits of a more considered mix of teachers, other professionals and ancillary staff at various levels within the establishment (NCE, 1993a; O'Neill, 1994a; Mortimore, Mortimore with Thomas, 1994).

The expectation that teachers alone should be the focus of human resource management in schools and colleges presents three significant difficulties for us.

1. It reinforces the historical notion that teachers can and should do everything, rather than concentrate on their most important professional role responsibility as managers of the learning process.

2. It focuses on the teacher rather than the tasks which need to be done in terms of managing and supporting student learning.

3. It fails to recognise other adults as significant and valuable members of teams which are structured to manage and support the learning process in a variety of ways.

As Bush and Middlewood (1997, p. ix) argue, in justifying the title of their book as *Managing People in Education*, distinguishing between different groups would 'negate the principle that all people are entitled to effective and sensitive management'.

A model for HRM in education

An HRM perspective which acknowledges the potential contributions of all adults employed within the institution has many benefits, not least because, for us, it incorporates each of the key terms in our original premise.

A broader definition of the term **people** is inclusive rather than exclusive. Holland (1998) claims that one of the key aims for education in the twenty-first century must be to be inclusive, not exclusive – for all members of society. It suggests that each adult employed within the school or college plays a critical role in its success. Acknowledging the unique contribution of individuals engenders **commitment**. Equally it focuses managerial attention on the **quality** of people needed and how those people can most effectively be encouraged and empowered to work together as part of an effective team. The sharing of work amongst team members is informed by an analysis of which tasks need to be done. In turn, support for team members and their work suggests that clear objectives need to be established and agreed, against which **performance** can be monitored, measured and evaluated.

Yourself in this HRM context

The idealistic, rational approach to the management of staff which we have just outlined may appear very remote from your own managerial experience in school or college. Before we proceed further, it may be a useful exercise for you to reflect on your own experience of being 'managed' in school or college, and, if appropriate, your experience of managing other adults.

Activity

Make brief notes upon the following questions:

How would you characterise the way other people manage you in school or college?

What are your positive experiences of being managed by others?

What are your negative experiences of being managed by others?

What are your feelings about our **premise**, outlined above, for the unit?

What are your feelings about our **model**, outlined above, for HRM in schools and colleges?

As a manager, what characterises the way you manage other staff?

❑ Comment

The way you manage others is likely to be informed by your own experience of being managed. These experiences may be positive or negative. You may be fortunate to work with colleagues whose management style provides positive role models and which you would like to emulate. Equally, you may have had negative experiences to date and be determined to manage others differently so that they do not suffer in the way that you feel you have done! Whatever your experiences to date we hope that your study of this unit will enable you to reflect on your previous and current practice and inform any strategies you adopt and action you take in the future.

Practice varies from organisation to organisation. It is likely, however, that you will have identified the importance of:

- commonly agreed and shared values within the working community, expressed through consistently applied management practices
- the imperative to make the most efficient use of scarce resources
- management processes which enable personal and institutional objectives to be balanced.

3. What is HRM?

HRM in the management world

This section considers:

- The growth of HRM
- The different approaches to HRM

Human resource management is generally agreed to have emerged into common usage within management vocabularies during the 1980s. There is still some difference of opinion regarding the acceptability of HRM as a generic term for the management and development of staff within organisations. This section explores the differences between the two terms 'HRM' and 'personnel management'. We examine the reasons for the emergence of HRM as an apparently distinctive approach to the management of staff in organisations. We also consider arguments from sources which articulate a certain scepticism about the actual contribution of HRM to organisational effectiveness.

❑ Origins of HRM

The term 'human resource management' (HRM) began to appear regularly in mainstream management terminology during the 1980s (for a chronological overview see Goss, 1994). In essence the term is intended to offer a broader, strategic and more dynamic interpretation of the role of effective staff management in organisations than had been the norm in previous decades. Amongst proponents of HRM approaches, 'personnel management' carries largely negative connotations.

❑ From personnel management to HRM

The move towards HRM approaches is attributable to the notion that traditional, specialist personnel provision:

- is unsustainably expensive in financial and human terms
- is highly bureaucratic
- leads to lengthy delay between identification of need and intervention
- offers solutions which work in artificial or simulated situations but are difficult to apply in the workplace
- threatens the relationship between line manager and subordinate
- is reliant on, and perpetuates the mystique of, the perceived expertise of personnel specialists rather than focusing on the development of line manager capability

❑ Human resource management

HRM approaches typically contain the following features. They:

- measure actions against the strategic objectives of the organisation as a whole
- emphasise the central importance of the line manager
- advocate customised, individual responses to intervention
- focus on positive motivation rather than negative control
- use process rather than standardised procedures
- are considered proactive rather than reactive
- are fully integrated into the day-to-day management of the organisation
- encourage purposeful negotiation and the resolution of potential conflict between manager and managed.

Table 3.1 *'Hard' and 'soft' approaches to management*

'Hard'	'Soft'
Systems-led	People-led
Market-led	
Cost-effectiveness	Effective learning
Unproblematic goals	Diverse goals, 'visions'
Periphery workers = variable costs	All workers important
Selection to 'fit'	Something to offer
Targeted development	Development for all
'Accountable' appraisal	'Development' appraisal
Human *resources*	*Resourceful* humans
People – means to an end	People – end in themselves
Control, compliance, 'fit'	Consensualism, mutuality, commitment
Training for now	Development for the future
Strategic concern	Excellence ethos
Mechanistic	'Organic'
Uniformity	Flexibility

(Hall, 1997a, p. 145)

HRM theory is predicated on the principles of concern for the quality of relationships, a desire to reduce unnecessary bureaucracy and a concern to see staff management issues as the routine preserve of the line manager, to be addressed in the workplace.

Fowler (1988, p. 1) in applying the HRM approach to a local government context, makes two key points relevant to our context:

- people are the primary resource
- human resource management is a prime responsibility of all managers, not a specialist role.

The debate between personnel management and HRM, as described by O'Neill (1994a, pp. 200–5), is less relevant now. Much more significant for managers in schools and colleges is an understanding of the philosophies of managing people (Hall, 1997a) which underpin particular approaches to HRM. The distinction between 'hard' and 'soft' approaches, although simplistic, does offer managers an insight into alternative strategies (see Table 3.1).

The impetus therefore for an increased focus on HRM approaches in the last decade or more demonstrates a high degree of similarity between the performance priorities of educational and other types of organisation (Riches and Morgan, 1989), together with a growing realisation that optimum, rather than merely adequate, levels of organisational performance depend on the effective management of human resources (Bush and Middlewood, 1997).

❏ Building on key learning points

The changing context of self-management for schools and colleges has ensured that their managers consider HRM strategies.

- HRM approaches are considered highly normative; they emphasise staff motivation, commitment and involvement.
- HRM approaches rely on the active participation of line managers.
- Personnel management approaches are seen as reactive and operationally oriented; HRM approaches are considered proactive and strategically oriented.
- HRM approaches provide a background against which the rapid and complex change within education can be managed.

 Reading

*Please read Tony Bush's chapter 'The changing context of management in education' in **Managing People in Education**, which describes how the world of education has changed, as has the world of work in society generally. This has had important consequences for the need for management in the educational world.*

HRM in education

This section considers:

- HRM specifically in the educational context
- the number of changes in this context which have influenced the changes in HRM in education.

❑ Introduction

In educational organisations the majority of personnel management functions have historically come within the remit of the local education authority (LEA) with the role of schools and colleges, until recently, being limited to the deployment of staffing establishments decided elsewhere. With the development of autonomous educational institutions the role of the institution has expanded rapidly in terms both of scope and complexity. Schools and colleges, however, face the additional challenge of coming to terms with the management implications of the HRM versus personnel management debate. In the further education (FE) sector, incorporation has meant that colleges, like grant-maintained (GM) schools, have full employer responsibilities and obligations (Warner and Crosthwaite, 1993). Within the maintained sector schools were faced with difficult decisions about which aspects of HRM administration and management can be managed well in-house and which need to be bought in as services from external agencies.

❑ Changes in HRM in education

The increased focus on the contribution of staff to organisational success is reflected, in England and Wales, in specific central government initiatives, designed to enhance teaching and management performance in autonomous schools and colleges:

- a broadening of entry routes into the teaching profession
- a strengthening of support arrangements for teachers at various career stages via
  - induction guidelines
  - mentoring schemes
  - attempts to develop taxonomies of professional and managerial competencies
- the introduction of appraisal schemes
- 'guided' funding for professional development activities
- the development of published performance indicators
- a preference for links between pay and performance (e.g. HMCI Report 1995)
- an enhanced focus on the role played by associate staff.

(O'Neill, 1994a, p. 205)

These initiatives are of major significance for the education service in several ways:

1.   The pattern of entry, or re-entry, to the teaching profession in the 1990s is fragmenting. This suggests that schools and colleges will need to develop flexible management responses to cope with an increasingly diverse group of recruits whose previous work experiences, career aspirations and needs in terms of personal and professional support will all vary considerably. Research suggests that the following factors will be of particular significance:

- From the mid-1990s demographic changes suggest a reduction in a 'pool' of well-qualified graduates leading to increased competition from staff from other sections. However, in the United Kingdom the potential effects of such demographic 'downturns' may be mitigated by factors such as the large increase in university entrance since 1988 but exacerbated by the low morale in the teaching profession, its 'poor image', and unattractiveness to potential recruits.

- Shortages of appropriately qualified teaching staff are likely to be subject-specific rather than across the board.

- The numbers of qualified but 'inactive' teachers are consistently identified (e.g. NCE, 1993a) as a potential, yet relatively untapped, source of supply.

- Over 400,000 teachers are currently employed in the maintained sector in England and Wales. Part-time employment accounts for less than 5 per cent of the total. There are over 350,000 people with teaching qualifications currently not employed in the maintained sector, over half of whom (200,000) are female, aged 30–49 (Buchan, Pearson and Pike, 1988, p. 1).

2.   The introduction of institutionally based modes of Initial Teacher Training (SCITT) implies that schools and colleges can seek to exercise more direct control over the style and type of initial training and the criteria which are used to select appropriate recruits at the point of entry to the profession. The premise for a revised, school or college-based, approach to teacher-training is twofold:

- Traditional 'instructional' teaching methods are inappropriate responses to the management of pupil or student learning in the 1990s and the next century. The role of the teacher in autonomous schools and colleges, prompted jointly perhaps by developments in information technology and greatly increased curriculum complexity, is moving towards that of 'facilitator' rather than 'deliverer' of education.

- In order to prepare new, and returning, teachers for this unfamiliar 'facilitator' role, a new type of training institution is necessary, one in which preferred good practice is modelled and encouraged for, as Holland (1998, p. 5) argues, 'the priority must be learning not teaching. Schools, colleges and universities are workplaces that have not changed much in decades. The world people are going to own and live in is not a world in which people sit neatly and tidily and change every hour from one subject to another. It is not a world of bits and pieces.'

3.   Documented, perennial difficulties caused by teacher wastage (Buchan, Pearson and Pike, 1988; NCE, 1993a), in particular in urban and inner city areas, imply that initial recruitment is not the only staff management issue facing schools and colleges. The introduction of induction guidelines, mentoring schemes and teacher appraisal frameworks imply that historically weak levels of institutional support for staff contribute in a substantive way to inappropriately high levels of teacher turnover. Blunkett's (1997) concern for the need for teachers to regularly update their professional skills and expertise links closely with a perceived need to deliver externally prescribed targets.

4.   Attempts to develop taxonomies of professional and managerial competences in education, and indeed to explicitly link pay and performance, reflect

   (a)   the increased awareness in all types of organisation of the importance of optimum employee involvement
   (b)   the need to identify appropriate standards of performance for individuals
   (c)   the importance of creating manageable agendas for individual employee development
   (d)   recognition of the value of early identification of potential for promotion.

The introduction in England and Wales of specific requirements based on prescribed standards, e.g. National Professional Qualifications for Headteachers (NPQH) and the proposed National Professional Qualification for Subject Leaders (NPQSL), indicates among other things a desire at national level to ensure value for money. This places pressure on schools and colleges to ensure similar value from their own staff and avoid unnecessary wastage either via avoidable staff turnover, or, just as significantly, from lack of motivation.

5.   A focus on staffing costs and levels of performance as major indicators of effective management within the organisation suggests that schools and colleges need to be creative in terms of their approaches to staffing curricular activities, so that:

- professional teacher expertise, which is expensive and may be in short supply, is employed directly in the management of student learning

- administrative or support activities are delegated where appropriate to non-teaching staff which, in general, costs less.

This shift in perspective, from 'supply' to 'demand' led staffing (O'Neill, 1994a), is reflected in tangible trends in schools and colleges. First, the use of large numbers of part-time staff in the further education sector (Fagg, 1991) demonstrated that at the time of incorporation many more teachers were being employed to staff certain viable curricular activities. In schools, the number of part-time qualified teachers had risen by 35.4 per cent in 1996 compared to 1989 (Select Committee, 1998). Secondly, the number of teachers in schools and colleges in a self-governing era who are on fixed-term contracts increased significantly in the 1990s. Thirdly, in both primary and secondary schools, budgetary autonomy has encouraged schools to scrutinise the distinction between teaching and non-teaching roles (Mortimore *et al.*, 1994). This has led to a broadening of the range and importance of activities undertaken by non-teaching staff, in both direct curriculum and more general managerial and administrative support (Mortimore *et al.*, 1994; Levacic, 1997). The number of non-teaching assistants in schools had risen by 51.25 per cent compared with 1989 (Select Committee, 1998).

6.   The creation of an educational marketplace, via the ERA and subsequent legislation, now has direct relevance for the recruitment of staff, just as much as students. With greater freedom to determine the range of benefits and working conditions on offer to individual staff comes the realisation that, particularly when seeking to attract quality staff institutions are in direct competition with each other (O'Neill, 1994a, p. 207).

There are three important management issues for schools and colleges here which arise directly from the move towards autonomous schools and colleges:

(a)   As *de facto* employers of staff, schools and colleges can exercise much greater degrees of latitude in terms of pay and conditions of service. As Fagg (1991) indicates, central government intention appears to be to urge employers, in the further and higher education sectors, to negotiate with staff on the basis of individual contracts wherever possible, leading eventually to the complete demise of collective bargaining and nationally determined norms.

(b)   One view of the impact of the shift of HRM responsibility from central to institutional organisations is that it inevitably led to school and college managers having to acquire 'more for less' from their workers (Ironside and Seifert, 1995). Since teachers are a labour intensive section (400,000 teachers at £11 billion in 1995), this view would see self-governance as ultimately being a rationalisation of cutting government costs. The consequences of 'more for less' may reveal themselves in high levels of stress and discontent (see the later section on 'stress').

(c)   Another effect of self-management has been the issue of affordability of staff. One way of keeping costs down is employing less experienced and therefore less expensive teachers. This practice may have consequences for job mobility. 'Older, more experienced and therefore more expensive teachers are finding job mobility and as a consequence promotion opportunities more difficult to come by' (Healy and Calveley, 1998, p. 20). This in turn can relate to staffroom dissent in the belief 'that they have been appointed not through achievement but simply as a cost factor' (ibid.).

The pace of change in the environment depends upon local conditions – the suburban or rural school, for example, is less likely to have problems in attracting staff. However, it may suffer from so much stability that the process of innovation and development may be hindered. Equally, any requirements for major retraining for existing staff may be a costly call on limited resources. These issues, however, are now part of the management brief of individual schools and colleges.

Schools and colleges, as autonomous institutions, need to develop highly customised HRM policies which reflect their own priorities in terms of recruiting, retaining and developing staff, rather than outdated national or local 'custom and practice'.

Schools and colleges need to consider the following in terms of developing their strategic approach to managing human resources (adapted from Armstrong, 1994):

Social responsibility – the philosophy of the organisation towards the people it employs, covering areas such as equity, consideration of individual needs and fears, the quality of working life.

Employment – the level of personnel the organisation wishes to employ, the provision of equal opportunity and reasonable security.

Pay – the level of pay and other benefits for employees and the extent to which pay systems are negotiated and disclosed.

Promotion – the attitude of the organisation to providing long-term career prospects and to promoting from within the organisation.

Training – the scope of training and staff development schemes and the extent to which the organisation proposes to subsidise education and training.

Industrial relations – policies on union recognition, closed shops, the role of teacher representatives and shop stewards and the approach to dealing with grievances, discipline and redundancy.

The key management issue which emerges for autonomous schools and colleges is the need to put in place policies for each of the above areas which reflect the aspirations, priorities and circumstances of the individual institution. These relate not only to the interpretation of statute in terms of employment law and equality of opportunity but also, and more significantly, to the broader ethical and social responsibility aspects of the employment and management of staff which distinguish one institution from another.

In England and Wales, more rigorous and regular inspection processes (Ofsted for schools and FEFC for colleges) may provide specific requirements for schools and colleges that are relevant. At the least, they may provide a framework within which staff can be managed to enable certain outcomes (e.g. of a post-inspection action plan) to be achieved.

Elliott and Hall (1994) express serious reservations about the incorporation of further education colleges in terms of the detrimental effects on the pay and conditions of service of teaching staff.

Armstrong's six areas for consideration provide a useful agenda for auditing both the spirit and the practice of human resource management policies within individual educational establishments.

Activity

Consider the six functions listed earlier by Armstrong in relation to your institution. For each function note:

- whether a policy exists
- how the policy was evolved
- who administers the policy
- who maintains the records and copes with administration.

What do your findings suggest about the 'hidden costs of autonomy'?

❏ Comment

Your answers to the above questions depend to a large extent upon the scale of operation of your school or college and the frequency with which individual functions are undertaken. Although larger organisations, such as FE colleges, are able to create their own specialist personnel function that deals with, for example, payment of salaries, this may be costly. Smaller schools and colleges experience problems in developing and maintaining specialist areas of personnel knowledge and expertise and in finding the time to undertake the work. Overall, however, the involvement of governors and senior staff in these functions can result in difficulties if a clear distinction between the creation of policy and day-to-day administration is not maintained.

❏ Building on key learning points

- As 'service' organisations, schools and colleges depend for their success on the commitment and capability of staff. This dependence is reflected in the increased use of public domain performance indicators for teaching and support staff.

- Flexible and creative use of associate staff and an awareness of the implications of the use of part-time staff and fixed-term contracts can be an important part of current HRM strategies in individual schools and colleges.

- Autonomous schools and colleges enjoy greater freedom and responsibilities in all areas of HRM as a result of which they are able to develop customised approaches to the management of staff, geared to the needs and circumstances of the individual institution.

◉ Reading

Please read John O'Neill's chapter, 'Managing human resources', pp. 206–18 in **Principles of Educational Management**, *which covers some of these issues in detail at the time when schools and colleges were beginning to become accustomed to self-governance.*

4. The management implications

People and performance

> This section considers:
>
> - several different approaches to performance management
> - the factors, especially support and motivation, which influence performance.

❏ Introduction

The period since 1979, in England and Wales, has seen the development of frameworks for the inspection of school and college performance, taxonomies of professional and managerial competence and comparative data in the form of published performance indicators for FEs, league tables of standardised assessment tests (SATs) and public examination results. The curricula which schools and colleges are required to deliver are either prescribed via statutory national curriculum (NC) programmes of study or, in the case of vocational curricula, determined by funding and validating bodies. Performance standards for autonomous schools and colleges, it may be argued, are increasingly centrally controlled by national government or government appointed quango. You will have noticed, no doubt, that your personal observations on your own teaching and managerial performance are increasingly measured against a framework of external expectations of performance. In addition, students and parents are encouraged to choose between competitor institutions on the basis of comparisons of actual and expected levels of performance rather than on the content of the curriculum.

At the same time, studies of management effectiveness in mainstream (e.g. Senge, 1990) and educational organisations (e.g. Grace, 1995; Jenkins, 1997) suggest that effective management is characterised by an ability and willingness to devolve authority and responsibility throughout the organisation so that individuals and teams are 'empowered' to act.

The philosophical and empirical bases for these exhortations reflect the notion that uniquely bureaucratic styles of management with their tight control and detailed assessments of performance are unlikely to secure optimum levels of staff performance.

Advocates of people-oriented management approaches (Riches, 1997) argue for supportive yet challenging styles of management. These are perceived as particularly appropriate in professionally staffed schools and colleges and a necessary response to curriculum and administrative overload in autonomous institutions.

This section examines the issues which confront managers in education in terms of responding to conflicting pressures for increased levels of public accountability and an appropriate degree of professional autonomy.

❏ Performance-centred approaches

The appearance of frameworks for the analysis of teaching or management performance reflects the trend in education towards more public or market-oriented forms of accountability. Bush (1994) analyses recent changes in the balance of accountability in education. His commentary demonstrates that, in particular since the 1988 Education Reform Act, there has been a substantive *increase* in the accountability of schools and colleges to external stakeholders. Such increases have been paralleled by a *diminution* in the scope, relevance and perceived importance of professional forms of accountability. The shift is significant. It not only reflects a more active role for central government and parents, as customers, in the definition of appropriate standards and the scrutiny of actual levels of performance, but also emphasises what sociologists of education, in particular, have called the attempted 'proletarianisation' of teaching (e.g. Healy and Kraithman, 1994). In this teachers are seen primarily as 'technicians' whose job is to implement closely defined curricula which have been determined elsewhere rather than as active professionals who are regarded, like other professions, as self-determining, self-regulating, self-monitoring and self-managing. The 'technician' analogy is most acute in the further education sector where the Further Education Funding Council (FEFC) and Training and Enterprise Councils (TECs) are seen to 'commission' the delivery of accredited vocational courses at regional and local levels with funding linked, at least in part, to successful student outcomes. Similar analogies may be drawn in relation to the development of the National Curriculum in England and Wales.

Below we briefly consider four perspectives on performance oriented approaches. These are:

- management by objectives
- managerial competences
- inspection frameworks
- value-added measures.

They differ in the extent to which performance standards in each approach are:

(a) internally generated
(b) customised
(c) developmentally oriented
(d) confidential.

(i) Management by objectives (MBO)

Squire (1989) argues that MBO provides an objective and necessary bulwark against both imposed performance standards and subjective or hearsay assessments of performance. For Squire MBO is essentially 'a system within which to carry out one's intentions' (p. 20), involving:

1. performance goals or targets initiated periodically by the employee

2. mutual agreement on a set of goals by the employee and his (sic) superior after discussion

3. periodic review by the employee and his superior of the match between goals and achievements.

Clearly the framework is skeletal in management terms. In relation to the work of schools and colleges there is no indication of how tensions between individual, team and whole institution objectives might be reconciled. Nor is there any reference to tangible support for training and development needs which arise from the target-setting process. Nevertheless, the language of the framework is indicative of an attempt to address the issues contributing to potential antipathy we discussed earlier. In that sense 'the approach is readily applicable in the education sector because, used appropriately, it values both professional "voice" and managerial responsibility' (O'Neill, 1994a, p. 217).

(ii) Managerial competences

If MBO can be defined as an internal institutional vehicle for agreeing targets and measuring progress towards meeting those targets, then the managerial competences movement offers a different perspective on the management of performance because it relies on a, largely external, detailed analysis of the *tasks* which might be carried out by people at various levels of responsibility within the 'typical' school or college. Task analysis is also perceived to help identify differences in levels of performance from, say, adequate to outstanding. The analysis leads to a statement of tasks or competences against which individual or team performance and quality of performance might be measured. Earley (1993) implies that, whilst the competences are deemed to be derived from, and relate to, actual workplace activities, the approach offers considerable possibilities when used for developmental rather than accountability purposes:

- it emphasises workplace performance
- it establishes an infrastructure which encourages and enables development to take place
- it is driven by practitioners rather than trainer providers
- it allows for better identification of training and development needs
- it provides a higher profile for career or personal development planning
- it empowers and motivates individuals to use the standards in ways which reflect their own needs and those of the schools in which they work
- it enables external inputs to be identified and tailored to an individual's or a school's development plan (Earley, 1993, p. 110).

However, 'tasks' is a limiting conception of competences, and subsequent developments of the approach (e.g. NPQH) have raised debates about the analysis also of traits, abilities and attributes as relevant.

Detailed studies for posts at various levels including headship (e.g. Jurasinghe and Lyons, 1996) strongly support the approach for development purposes. Whilst the approach is seen to have some advantages, critics argue that at an operational level it is time-consuming and expensive both to set up and to administer, and generic rather than customised in its approach. More significantly, perhaps, competences are seen as a problematic vehicle for identifying or developing the higher order, creative, adaptive management skills which will be at a premium in autonomous schools and colleges. As Ouston (1993, p. 217) notes, 'if the model is very skills based, rather than qualities based, it is likely to reflect the present rather than the future.'

(iii) Inspection frameworks

In England and Wales, both the inspection authorities (Ofsted and FEFC) encapsulate attempts to define generic criteria against which performance might be assessed both within and between institutions.

> The purpose of inspection is to identify strengths and weaknesses in schools so that they may improve the quality of education offered and raise the standards achieved by their pupils. Particular attention is paid to pupils' standards of achievement which are better or worse in any subject or area of learning than the average for their age and to reasons for such differences (Ofsted, 1995, p. 4).

The emphasis of the framework is on the contribution of teaching and management to enhanced educational outcomes whilst the criteria explicitly focus on norm-referenced standards of student attainment. In this sense staff performance is evaluated in terms of 'the quality of teaching provided and its effects on the quality of learning and standards of pupils' achievements' (ibid., p. 27). Since 1997, in England and Wales, individual teachers have been graded for their classroom performance. The perspective is clearly one of external accountability in which priority is given to educational attainments, or outcomes, rather than to the process of teaching and learning in its own right. In Drucker's (1988) terms the quality of education is measured according to results not good intentions. However, assessments of performance which are based purely on raw data or normative criteria can be misleading.

Riches (1997, p. 17) summarises the basic problems which need to be considered before human performance can be understood:

1. The reliability of performance or consistency or stability over time. Are the best (or worst) performers at time 1 the best or (worst) performers at time 2? Psychological evidence indicates that this is not necessarily so because people are inconsistent in their performances or conditions in which the performances take place may vary (Cascio, 1991).
2. The reliability of job performance observations in which different methods may result in markedly different conclusions about performance.
3. The dimensionality of job performance: a great variety of predictors can be used but most empirical studies and people in practice use only a global measure or criterion (Ronan and Prien, 1971).
4. In performance the moderating effects of situational variables, such as organisational characteristics or leadership influences, invariably come into play.

Another critical comment to be made concerns the weight, or relative importance, of the various components within any one assessment of performance system. How is it decided, and who decides, which one is more important than another?

These general points are made to demonstrate that there is a good deal of subjectivity surrounding the evaluation of performance. A system of performance-related pay, for instance, would need to be based upon an assessment of performance in which all potential recipients had confidence.

(iv) Value-added measures

The argument for value-added approaches to the measurement of teaching and management effectiveness relates to the, quite logical, notion that student attainment, whether on entry to formal schooling at 4+ or on completion at 16, is extremely varied. In this sense the use of raw data to measure institutional or individual teacher effectiveness is too crude an approach. Hence there is the need to develop procedures which assess attainment on entry in order to measure 'distance travelled' by students, rather than simply linking effectiveness with student outcomes. Such procedures are 'achieved through sophisticated statistical modelling, allowing only for those variables which can be consistently measured across all schools and which can be relatively objectively assessed' (Schagen and Morrison, 1997, p. 1).

However, the difficulties of applying value-added approaches to the assessment of staff performance are considerable. They also create the potential for disenfranchisement of certain categories of student:

> For a number of management functions within a school or college, including staff appraisal, it is useful to know whether an abnormal level of achievement by students is partially explained by the students' prior ability. And if performance-related pay is introduced for teachers and lecturers, the use of value-added evaluations may help prevent perverse effects. If performance-related pay were determined without reference to initial attainment, teachers and lecturers with less promising intakes would receive less bonus than their counterparts in other schools or colleges. This would make teachers and lecturers less willing to work with less promising students, and institutions serving such students would become doubly disadvantaged (Ofsted and Audit Commission, 1993, pp. 64–5).

Activity

Consider the extent to which the four possible performance-centred approaches are used within your school or college. For what particular purposes are the various approaches used? List the advantages and disadvantages of each approach as used within your institution.

❑ Comment

Most schools and colleges are likely to use a combination of approaches, either by coincidence or by design. The effectiveness of each approach, and the extent to which it is used, depends on:

- its acceptability to the staff concerned
- the availability of valid and reliable data to inform assessments
- an understanding of the ways in which performance may be enhanced via assessment.

◉ Reading

Please read Colin Riches' chapter 'Managing for people and performance' in **Managing People in Education**, *pp. 15–22. This explores the notion of HRM values and processes underpinning all aspects of the management of people in schools and colleges.*

❏ People-oriented approaches

Elliott and Hall (1994) offer a critique of the way in which, in their view, 'hard' HRM approaches, which categorise people as just another resource to be manipulated in pursuit of organisational objectives, have apparently been adopted with enthusiasm by senior managers within the further education sector, post-incorporation. They point to deteriorating conditions of service for full-time staff and potential exploitation of hourly-paid staff as indicators of an inappropriate emphasis on outcomes, or performance, at the expense of people.

Similarly, Hoyle and Jones (1995) argue that control over teachers has become more overt, 'helped by the rise of managerialism as a significant force at the school level' (p. 74). At the same time, the emergence of educational institutions as wild or open organisations which have to compete and survive in an increasingly turbulent economic, demographic and educational environment reinforces our basic premise (p. 5) that schools and colleges depend for their success on the people who work there. People-oriented, as opposed to performance-oriented, perspectives may be likened to a 'soft' HRM approach, which suggests a 'spirit which values employees as human beings and enables them to do extraordinary things' (Riches, 1997, p. 17).

In addition, the general move towards HRM approaches, with a consequent emphasis on the role of the line manager, has considerable implications for the development of higher order interpersonal and communication skills in all types of organisation (O'Neill, 1994b). In schools and colleges, particularly in the light of trends towards flexible, independent and life-long student learning, these skills are at a premium not only in staff–staff relationships, but also in interactions between staff and students, and between staff and the host of other stakeholders who form part of the institution's educational community.

(i) The importance of motivation

In our introduction we set out our understanding of the symbiotic relationship between individual performance and organisational effectiveness. We also suggested that optimum levels of commitment and performance were entirely contingent on management effectiveness: commitment and performance have to be actively managed rather than simply be assumed or left to chance. Underpinning this notion of affecting and improving the performance capability of individuals is the concept of motivation. Riches (1994a) implies that the concept is multi-faceted and, as such, eludes satisfactory definition. Nevertheless, he argues, the importance of motivation to autonomous schools and colleges lies both in the recognition that people are the key resource and in an awareness that training and development are key elements in promoting enhanced levels of motivation amongst, and contributions from, staff. For a detailed consideration of the importance of motivation, please see the later section on this topic.

It is significant that, in linking motivation to management strategies, Riches highlights challenging goals, adequate support and training and feedback on performance as essential elements for promoting job satisfaction. Each of these, as we discuss later, is an important part of effective schemes for the induction, mentoring and appraisal of staff.

People-oriented approaches are significant in educational management because they advocate the use of a range of motivational strategies depending on the needs of the individual. For some those needs will be satisfied by purely pecuniary rewards, for others responsibility and autonomy will act as motivating factors, for yet others it will be regular and tangible recognition of performance within the team which will be paramount. For some teachers the prospect of negotiating individual job descriptions and performance targets with performance-related pay will be an appealing prospect. For others the quality of welfare, grievance and professional association support will impact significantly on their perceptions about the quality of their working environment. O'Neill (1994a) identifies a range of factors which are available to individual institutions to respond to the needs of individuals and groups of staff within the school or college. These are shown in Figure 4.1.

Equally people-oriented approaches acknowledge the extrinsic nature of motivation in that it depends on feedback and support from others within the team or wider institution. The key management issues may

Remuneration	Welfare	Development
Starting salary	Incapacity benefits	Induction
Salary progression	Career-break entitlements	Mentoring
Performance-related pay	Child-care provision	Appraisal
	Security of tenure	Opportunities for career and
	Grievance and discipline mechanisms	professional development
	Counselling	
	Working conditions	
	Union recognition	
	Redundancy	

Figure 4.1   Factors in the management of staff commitment (O'Neill, 1994a, p. 215)

therefore be those of (a) the appropriate management style and (b) a structure which enables this support and feedback at all levels through a teams-based approach.

(ii) Implications for managers in schools and colleges

We conclude this section with an assessment of the issues which need to be addressed by schools and colleges in their attempts to resolve the people versus performance debate. We end this section by returning to the management of learning implications of the debate.

1. Drucker (1988, p. 362) argues that the guiding principle for any policy or action in the management of staff has to be that of integrity; decisions which relate to the management of staff have to be consistent with the values espoused by the institution, and not, by implication, governed by considerations of expediency. This is a significant polemic in educational management because schools and colleges are subject to powerful external financial and accountability constraints which, at times, conflict with historical staffing structures and accepted norms concerning conditions of service. There are considerable potential hazards in a management approach which emphasises efficiency and outcomes at the expense of individual welfare. Equally, however, Drucker explicitly links integrity with a concern for high performance standards. Inappropriate standards of performance, he suggests, should not be ignored but must be actively confronted and addressed, so that organisations develop a norm of high expectations of performance and achievement.

2. Riches (1997, p. 17) points out the inevitable subjectivity involved in assessing performance standards that are dependent on context and a host of organisational and environmental variables which militate against the simplistic comparison of performance both within and between institutions. At the heart of the process of defining performance standards lies the issues of ownership and fitness-for-purpose, i.e. whether the performance is of the appropriate quality to achieve what is required.

❑ **Building on key learning points**

- External forms of accountability and published performance standards are routine aspects of the management of autonomous schools and colleges; studies of management effectiveness suggest that empowerment and autonomy for staff are important contributors to internal organisational effectiveness.

- An insistence on high standards of performance and a concern for the differing needs of individual staff are complementary, rather than conflicting, aspects of the effective management of human resources.

- Optimum levels of individual performance are contingent upon effective management which is characterised by support, feedback on performance and higher order interpersonal skills.

- Individual motivation to perform is informed and constrained by an understanding of organisational values and norms.

 Reading

You have already read the first part of Colin Riches' chapter, in Managing People in Education. Now, please read the remainder, pp. 22–8, which shows how the underlying values balancing concern for people and performance can apply to managerial processes.

The individual and the organisation

This section considers:

- how individual and organisational development need to be integrated
- some of the issues affecting this integration.

❑ Introduction

The existence of a causal relationship between optimum individual performance and an effective framework of organisational support is central to the principles of human resource management. Whilst the management of classroom teaching and learning at the point of delivery may, in your experience, be largely a solitary professional role, the broader range of administrative and managerial tasks which you undertake within the institution are collaborative activities; you will normally work as a member of one or more groups or teams in the pursuit of common objectives.

Professional development in this context will be part of that framework of organisational support, the objective of which is to help integrate the development of individuals within the work of the organisation.

(i) The importance of integration

There are several reasons which help to explain the emergence of integration as a key management issue in both individual and organisational development.

1. In autonomous schools and colleges, traditional staffing structures and historical divisions between professional and other types of work are increasingly being called into question (e.g. Saran and Busher, 1995).

2. External accountability and resource efficiency factors have led to organisations in all sectors being less tolerant of what Riches (1994a) labels organisational 'slack', thus schools and colleges are exhorted to ensure appropriate levels of contribution from all individuals and groups within the organisation. The emphasis on target-setting (e.g. DfEE, 1995) reinforces the notion of minimum requirements for the institution and the individuals who work in it.

3. The increasing complexity of the management of learning in the 1990s, reflected in the use of a more diverse range of teaching and learning styles, rapid developments in the content and skills specifications for areas of learning and greater sophistication in the assessment and recording of individual student learning, creates significant organisational difficulties in terms of managers attempting to simultaneously support individual, curriculum and whole institution development.

4. The massive increase in information processing demanded of autonomous schools and colleges, combined with the very real need for higher order interpersonal and communication skills in working relationships, serve to underline the importance of effective communication networks and procedures in educational organisations. In this sense the concept of integration embraces both the relationships between people within the school or college and the work they do.

We begin this part of the section by looking briefly at the range of tensions associated with organisational development identified by Dalin (1993), and then proceed to examine how the work of the school or college might be organised to facilitate such integration and development. The relationship between teamwork and development is analysed in depth. The latter parts of the section consider issues associated with the management of accountability and development.

(ii) Organisational development

Dalin's extensive work on institutional development in northern Europe, principally in Norway, the Netherlands and Germany, has identified effective human relations between all members of the school community as a key determinant of school quality. Certain institutional 'dilemmas' are enumerated:

- How can 'membership' really be felt, even when personal values, personality and norms are different from those of the majority?
- How are feelings expressed? Can a school accept all forms of feelings (and their expression)? And how can one be fair? (For example, do we treat boys and girls alike?)
- Do we accept that all members, students as well as leaders, have the right to influence, and how can we deal with unacceptable ways of using influence (by leaders, teachers and students)?
- Does the school have an open and constructive communication process at all levels, or is energy blocked because people do not talk to each other?
- How does the school deal with conflicts and problem-solving? Does it have acceptable procedures and norms or are these ad hoc or non-existent?
- Is the school working with its own culture and climate, and are 'process' issues accepted, as well as discussions of content? (Dalin, 1993, p. 9)

These management dilemmas, albeit expressed in 'broadwash' terms, provide a useful agenda for individual and organisational development from an HRM perspective. In particular they reinforce the importance of the following issues:

- appropriate and effective **communication** processes
- full **integration** of all organisational members
- positive **resolution of conflict**
- a **code of conduct** which reflects the organisation's **culture**
- appropriate degrees of **involvement in decision-making**.

Such issues are complex in terms of overall school and college management. Decisions, for example, about the form and content of induction, mentoring and appraisal schemes may challenge existing values and norms within the institution.

However, integration occurs as individuals take on meaningful work within various groups within the institution. Individual and organisational development are seen to be symbiotic:

- the common **process** is effective group or teamwork
- the **critical success factor** in terms of organisational development is the linking together of the work of different operating units (see Figure 4.2).

Everard and Morris (1990) argue that it is at the level of inter-team practice that communication networks and procedures are most significant, whilst within individual teams consensus around goals, purposeful leadership and higher-order interpersonal skills are called for. These latter issues are discussed in the later section on a teams-based approach.

Official integration occurs through induction and mentoring schemes, existing departmental team structures, membership of working groups, and cross-school or college groups involved with the management of, for example, pastoral care, assessment and record-keeping or student support. Unofficial integration may well arise from friendship networks and voluntary activities such as a school trip or fund-raising event. It is important to realise that the way individuals and groups develop within the institution will be influenced by both official and unofficial processes. Equally it is important to note that integration

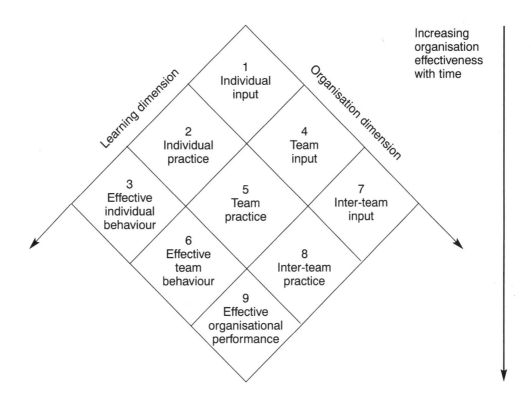

Figure 4.2 **Training and organisation development matrix (Everard and Morris, 1990, p. 173)**

and development can, and do, take place outside formal training programmes. This consideration of the whole picture or culture of the organisation is discussed in the later section on culture.

(iii) Organisational size and complexity
Empirical studies in schools in England and Wales have demonstrated the difficulties, in particular, of ensuring the integration of different teams within the one organisation.

> One of the criteria by which senior staff identified effective middle managers, and a quality which was highly valued, was the ability to take a wide perspective and see subject or area concerns in the context of the whole school. Middle managers who fought for their own corner regardless of the needs of colleagues in other departments and whole school policies were regarded unfavourably (Earley and Fletcher Campbell, 1992, p. 192).

This notion is reinforced by Bolam *et al.* (1993) whose study of management practice in primary and secondary schools emphasised the importance of organisational **size** and **complexity** as contributory factors to the level of integration and general organisational effectiveness.

> Primary schools have relatively small and simple structures which are probably relatively easy to co-ordinate, whereas secondary schools are relatively large, complex and less easy to co-ordinate at school level, but probably more tightly structured and easier to co-ordinate at department level. It may well be the case, therefore, that primary headteachers and teachers are more likely to have a shared understanding of the various aspects of school management than their secondary colleagues, whereas the latter are more likely to have that understanding at departmental level. There was some evidence that subject departments were the key management structures in secondary schools but there was little evidence of inter-departmental collaboration (Bolam *et al.*, 1993, pp. 124–5).

In their study of effective and ineffective departments in secondary schools, Sammons, Thomas and Mortimore (1997) found that different departments even within the same school achieved markedly differently. While they identified a number of factors contributing to the effectiveness of individual departments, the one that is most relevant here was the quality of the Senior Management Team's leadership, particularly in the relationship between the SMT and the Heads of Departments.

Activity

List those features of size and complexity which help and hinder integration of the various working units within your school or college. What would now be your priority for action?

❏ Comment

You will perhaps have concluded that numbers of staff, their relative physical isolation from each other, timetable arrangements and competing work demands are negative aspects of size which hinder both development work and more general integration. The great advantage of size is that it can provide some economies of scale in terms of management and administration.

The features of complexity you have identified may be related to competition for resources, interpersonal or group relationships and management or organisational structures. Your priority for action might be the most significant issue or, conversely, the most readily changed feature. But which would be the most effective?

(iv) Organisational improvement and individual development

Implicit throughout our discussions in this section has been the argument that individual and organisational development are closely intertwined. This is evident in the normative matrix provided by Everard and Morris (p. 25) which is conceptually useful but fails to acknowledge the difficulties of integrating the work of individuals within teams or of marrying the priorities of various teams within the institution. The polemic returns us to the arguments we originally discussed in relation to the HRM versus personnel management debate. In the context of educational organisations, is individual development the responsibility of the individual, the professional tutor, the team leader or the institution as a whole?

Up to the late 1980s, it could be argued that the management of individual performance was routinely characterised by evaluation and target-setting mechanisms, but lacked any systematic approach to support for the work of the individual:

> All the emphasis is on evaluation with some on performance planning but very little, if any, attention is directed towards coaching or supporting and helping employees win (Blanchard and Peale, 1988, p. 100).

The School Management Task Force (SMTF) for England and Wales argued for support and encouragement being at the heart of effective development of school leaders and managers.

Day (1995, p. 123) argues the case for 'active encouragement of critical friendships which may be defined as practical partnerships entered voluntarily, based upon a relationship between equals and rooted in a common task or shared concern'. Such friendships decrease isolation and through stages move the individual from reflection to confrontation of, for example, the need for changes in practice. Among the advantages of critical friends listed by Day (1995) are:

- being used to check against bias in self-reporting
- contribute to policy development
- act as a resource which teachers and others may use at times appropriate to the needs perceived.

The key responsibility for developing such communities within which these friendships prosper lies with leaders, according to Day (1995).

(v) A coherent human resource strategy

A strategic perspective of managing human resources in the school or college is essential if the performance of the individual is to be successfully integrated into the essential focus upon organisational effectiveness. Three broad coherent human resource strategies may be described, each of which has implications for organisational leadership and management.

1. **Inducement Strategy**. This approach relates effective individual performance to being achieved through motivation by reward (and the opposite). Organisations pursing this strategy may have features of restrictive role behaviour and job descriptions, selection on the basis of narrow, highly specified requirements and management would tend to be controlled or supervisory.

2. **Investment Strategy.** Organisations following this strategy emphasise staff development and expect employees to exercise some initiative and creativity in carrying out tasks. Key values would be personal growth, justice, security and respect.

3. **Involvement Strategy**. Autonomy and responsibility would be at the heart of organisations following this strategy. Staff would be expected to show flexibility, to adapt to change as well as demonstrate considerable initiative. Team-based work would be central and management's supervision would be facilitative.

Sivasubramanian and Ratnam (1998), in their study of companies in India, suggested that inducement strategy appeared to be most suitable when *efficiency* was seen as the key to success. Investment strategy was most applied where *service differentiation* (making the organisation 'special') was needed. Involvement strategy was best suited where the need was for *continuous innovation and high quality*.

In the current context of self-managing schools and colleges, managers of human resources may find it helpful to explore the notion of which strategy is most likely to enable them to deliver the goals required of them. The fact that these goals may be increasingly decided centrally can be a significant factor in determining the extent to which autonomy and empowerment are possible. What is certain is that the integration of individual effort and performance with the overall effectiveness of the organisation remains the key quest for HR managers.

Activity

Which of the three HRM strategies above do you see most evidence of in your own organisation? List the specific areas of HRM management which seem most relevant to your evidence.

(vi) Developments in training

The School Management Task Force report (DES, 1990) provides a concise chronology of the changes in management development approaches in education. In particular they focus on:

- a move away from knowledge-based, off-site courses
- a more explicit linkage between training or development and actual work undertaken
- the managerial support that institutions need to provide as a matter of course for individuals in the workplace.

The change of emphasis is illustrated in Figure 4.3.

Current emphasis	Redirected emphasis
Tutor-directed courses	Support for self-directed study by individuals, school teams, peer groups
Off-site training	In-school and near-to-the-school training
Predetermined times	Flexitime study
Oral presentations	Distance learning materials, information packs and projects
Provider-determined syllabus	School-determined agenda
Knowledge acquisition	Performance enhancement

Figure 4.3   Changing priorities in management training provision (DES, 1990, p. 21)

Their perspective reinforces the idea that individual and organisational development should be synonymous:

> It becomes possible to regard the achievement of corporate goals and meeting the individual's needs more as matters of mutual benefit than of competing demands. For example, succession planning to forecast job vacancies and to meet future organisational requirements can improve individual career opportunities. Recognition of the need to match corporate and individual needs results in a more sharply focused approach to the selection of learning opportunities of benefit to both. School management development seen from this perspective is directly related to the effectiveness of the school and its management, as well as to the experiences of teachers and pupils. It is no longer a marginal activity. Training and development activities must be planned and implemented in the broader context of the organisation (DES, 1990, pp. 8–9).

It is possible to draw on our discussions throughout this section and suggest that effective individual development requires the following preconditions to exist in schools and colleges:

- a strong and supportive organisational culture
- a clearly defined and accepted role for line managers or team leaders
- a review and development process which integrates the development of individuals within the routine work of the school or college.

❑ Building on key learning points

- Individual and organisational development are symbiotic; working in teams is likely to provide an effective vehicle for the development of both.

- Effective development is constrained by potential tensions in inter-team practice, definitions of the role of the line manager or team leader, and the closeness of the link between training and actual performance.

- Effective development is dependent on an appropriate process to support review together with higher order communication and interpersonal skills to promote meaningful analysis of practice.

- The ability of individuals and organisations to develop is determined by existing norms concerning institutional culture and the overall approach to managing human resources in the organisation.

Section B

5. Managing the school or college and its staff

Introduction

The first section took an overview in considering the role of managing people in educational organisations, and the different approaches which could be taken to human resource management. It established the importance of achieving the best possible performance from all who work within the school or college, and began to explore some general principles for managing people.

This section examines policy and practice in key areas. We open with consideration of an overarching concept, that of the learning organisation, and consider what such a concept may mean to a school or college and how it could be achieved. We then explore a number of areas which are critical to achieving successful performance: equal opportunities, motivation, and stress/time management. Finally we look at some of the ways in which people may work together, exploring how teams and teamwork could be achieved, the roles and structures within which people work, and in conclusion, the overall culture of an organisation and how it can contribute to performance. Overall, this section aims to suggest ways in which individuals and groups of people can be supported to give of their best, creating a synergy by working together effectively.

The concept of the learning organisation

This section considers:

- the reasons for interest in the concept of the learning organisation
- definitions of the concept
- the nature of learning
- steps to achieve a learning organisation.

❑ Interest in the concept

Interest in the concept of the learning organisation has grown steadily in both education and business since it was coined around 1988 (Jones and Hendry, 1994). The technology revolution and ever increasing demands on education have rendered incremental development an insufficient response. If the speed of innovation means that the problems and solutions of the past are no longer an adequate basis on which to plan, then new ways of coping with change are imperative. A change in approach which is qualitatively different may be needed. Put another way, new forms of learning are needed, and the concept of the learning organisation appears an enticing goal. Schools and colleges aspire to achieving such an organisation, not only because of a possible link between success in this area and school effectiveness (Sammons, Hillman and Mortimore, 1995) but also because of a commitment to demonstrate the centrality of learning in people's lives, as part of a learning community and learning society.

❑ Defining the learning organisation

The attractiveness of the concept may relate to a lack of precision in its definition. Some have attempted to describe a mix of factors which through synergy would lead to a learning organisation. The prescription includes variations of both particular characteristics of managers, such as flexibility, a moral and ethical approach, etc., and a range of structural features such as teamworking and linking individual development to organisational objectives (Beard, 1993). Other writers have viewed such definitions as superficial and unlikely to lead to transformation. They have focused on a more fundamental reconsideration of what the relationship between individual and organisational learning may be, and how learning is experienced (Jones and Hendry, 1994; West, 1994).

❏ Individual and organisational learning

West draws on Argyris and Schon (1978) to argue that simply increasing the amount of individual learning will not lead to a transformation of the organisation:

> There can be no organizational learning without individual learning, but the individual learning is a necessary but insufficient condition for organizational learning (West, 1994, p. 32).

Several writers explore the paradox that an abstract, 'the organisation', cannot learn, and yet the sum of individual learning may in some sense, under certain conditions, result in whole organisation evolution. The two key factors appear to be firstly that all individuals focus their learning on the same goal, or vision (Senge, 1990; West, 1994) and secondly that individual learning is communicated to others and sufficiently absorbed as to become embedded, that is, resulting in a consistent change in behaviour by a critical mass of people. The questions that arise are:

- How can all staff be helped to learn?
- How can that individual learning be shared and embedded?

❏ The nature of learning

Exploration of the process of learning in organisations suggests that even in schools and colleges where learning is central, staff learning may be blocked or happening in ways which are not helpful. As Honey asserts:

> People learn whether we want them to or not. The trouble is that most organisations are unwittingly designed to encourage the acquisition of behaviours and practices they wish they had less of (Honey, 1991, p. 30).

Jones and Hendry (1994) describe 'hidden learning' which is the unconscious adoption of norms, values and practice of the job. They further define learning using a 'second agenda':

> People know when to speak and when to keep quiet, they begin to understand how the communication and other social systems operate (Jones and Hendry, 1994, p. 157).

People may be adopting behaviours which perpetuate ineffective practice, inappropriately protecting others from confronting development needs, or preventing them personally from moving outside a comfort zone. Jones and Hendry argue that this learning which falls outside the formal systems for staff development is a critical feature, and that until understanding is increased of the role of culture and emotions in staff's learning and their subsequent performance, learning will continue to risk being inadequate or negative in its impact on the organisation.

Argyris (1991) goes further, and reasons that professionals, above all, become very skilled in resisting learning. He believes that the very success of professionals in achieving their position weakens their capacity to think critically of their own performance, to deal with criticism and mistakes, and to dismantle a faulty self-image which acts as a barrier between self and accurate self-assessment:

> Even if we feel uncertain or ignorant, we learn to protect ourselves from the pain of appearing uncertain or ignorant. That very process blocks out any new understandings which might threaten us. The consequence is what Argyris calls 'skilled incompetence' – teams full of people who are incredibly proficient at keeping themselves from learning (Senge, 1990, p. 25).

Argyris (1991) also argues that where learning occurs it may be too limited. He contrasts 'single-loop' learning, that is learning which compares progress with the agreed indicators of success and adjusts to keep things on track, with 'double-loop learning' where the goals and routes themselves, the definitions of success, are challenged and transformed. He suggests that failure in single-loop learning leads professionals to defensive behaviour with blame directed at other individuals and groups, or to inconsistency between what is declared and what is enacted:

> Teaching people how to reason about their behaviour in new and more effective ways breaks down the defences that block learning (Argyris, 1991, p. 100).

In other words, the first lesson of consideration of the concept of the learning organisation is that success in a career, even in education, is no guarantee of an ability to learn, and that staff may need a great deal more help than has previously been recognised in learning how to learn. The fast changing environment may have exacerbated the difficulties in achieving learning. Kelly (1995), researching the learning and management style of 310 school heads, deputies and middle managers in primary and secondary schools, suggested that the pressures experienced in the 1990s have led to a move away from reflection and analysis, and towards an activist approach to learning. School leaders were reacting rather than reflecting and planning. Drawing together all these concerns about the nature of learning in organisations, it is clear that staff development processes may need to focus not just on the area of development, whether it be classroom-based skills or management skills, but on the process of learning itself if they are to be effective.

Activity

You may wish to reflect on the quality and effectiveness of staff learning in your organisation. List the means by which individual learning is disseminated and shared. Assess whether the systems for sharing learning really engage staff. How far is the hidden learning referred to by Jones and Henry (1994) inhibiting learning? Ask colleagues if they feel free to openly discuss both positive and negative views of developments in the organisation.

❑ Achieving a learning organisation

A universal commitment to development and change cannot be assumed. Some may view a move to significant learning as deeply threatening:

> Whittington (1993) suggests that managers 'refuse to learn because they understand perfectly well the implications for their power and status.' Resistance to change may not be 'stupid' . . . but based on a very shrewd perception of the consequences (West, 1994, pp. 35–6).

Achieving learning may be therefore, as Garratt (1994) suggests, 'an essentially political process'. Before any consideration of how learning is taking place in an organisation can be achieved, a sufficient number of people must be persuaded of the necessity of such a process. Southworth (1994) in his study of 'The Learning School' concluded that the headteacher is the leading learner, and must establish the central focus on every level of learning from that of the pupils to all the staff, the organisation, and his or her own. Several writers including Argyris (1991), Garratt (1994) and Senge (1990) agree that establishing learning as central is a strategic imperative for the leader of any organisation. If creating commitment is the foundation, then alignment of goals is the next step:

> You cannot have a learning organization without shared vision. Without a pull toward some goal which people truly want to achieve, the forces in support of the status quo can be overwhelming. Vision establishes the overarching goal (Senge, 1990, p. 209). ✳

Achieving such a vision may be problematic (Foreman, 1997) but without it, learning may follow different paths in a number of directions, precluding the critical mass of changed behaviour needed to result in organisational and not just individual evolution. Holding in view a vision of what the goal of the organisation is, all staff can attempt to analyse and improve the quality of their learning, recognising the need to address the hidden as well as the overt. We take a more detailed look at staff development issues in the final section.

❏ **Building on key learning points**

- The definition of the concept of the learning organisation is varied and sometimes inexact, but it may nevertheless be a powerful ideal to guide action.

- The concept challenges some of the widely held beliefs of educational professionals, that they are good at learning, and that increasing individual development activity will necessarily develop the whole school or college.

- Aligning individual development goals against organisational strategic goals may not be the most important initial focus for staff development. Rather the headteacher or principal may need to focus on establishing a culture which allows people to analyse with others the holistic and bounded nature of their learning.

- Although this section has concentrated on the management of staff, the focus on learning to learn may be most effective when it is universally applied to students/pupils as well as all staff.

- The concept may not be appropriate to all schools and colleges. Political, cultural or external factors may indicate that it is not the moment to attempt this approach.

 Reading

*Jacky Lumby's chapter, 'The learning organisation', in **Managing People in Education**, offers a more detailed consideration of how the learning of individual staff can be supported and of the structural and process changes which may lead to the achievement of a learning organisation.*

Managing for equal opportunities

This section considers:

- the definition of equality of opportunity
- the importance of working towards equality of opportunity
- the current position in schools and colleges
- the causes of inequality
- possible ways forward.

Ask people working in education if they endorse equality of opportunity for both students and staff, and the vast majority would assert their wholehearted support. At the level of general concept, there is no problem in achieving consensus. But, as with many concepts in education, closer definition may uncover uncertainties and disagreement.

Perhaps the range of views of those working in education might reveal itself most strongly when people are asked what an educational institution which had achieved equality of opportunity would look like. Would the school or college have proportions of women and men, both overall and in senior positions, reflecting the percentages of each in the population, or the proportion employed in that educational phase? Would the number and diversity of minority ethnic staff reflect the local community or national demography?

Would the staff not necessarily display these statistical parallels, but simply be an outstanding group of people, indicating that recruitment ensured that the most talented and skilled were attracted and recruited, irrespective of gender, race or disability? Does managing for equality of opportunity mean all staff are treated the same, or according to their individual need? Does the latter imply treating some more favourably than others to overcome previous and/or current disadvantage?

Most people focus on the **inputs** of equality of opportunity, and may be proud of their policy documents, their training for interviewers, their on-site nurseries, etc. Fewer focus on the **outputs**, that is the indicators of success. Monitoring staff by ethnicity, gender and disability is the only current widespread measure of 'success'. This numerical approach to equal opportunities may relate to the legislative base within the UK, Europe and North America which does not attempt to radically change the organisations in which people work. Rather it takes an 'equal slice of the pie' approach, without questioning the nature of the pie. This implied definition of equality of opportunity has been criticised on two counts. Firstly, it defines success in terms of the current system, the values and practice of which may be unsatisfactory or even abhorrent to some. As Acker (1994) points out, more radical approaches using concepts such as racism, patriarchy and oppression are largely excluded from the discourse of education on equal opportunity. Secondly, it focuses managers on certain forms of discrimination, ignoring others. For example, Heasman (1993), writing of the experience of members of the National Association of Teachers in Further and Higher Education, argues that:

> The form of harassment and discrimination which affects the highest proportion of our members is ageism (to which we will all be subject in due course) (Heasman, 1993, p. 28).

Managing for equality of opportunity can be defined in a negative way as removing all forms of unfair discrimination, or positively, as attracting and using to the full the talents and experience of all parts of the community. It can be seen as minimalist complying with legal requirements, or as a radical attack on racism and patriarchy. Action which plans to move beyond a rhetorical commitment may find it useful to start with achieving individual and organisational clarity on what exactly not only the inputs but also the outputs of an equal system would be.

Activity

Write your own definition of equality of opportunity. Avoid generalisations and try to describe what success would look like, how you might measure it, and what changes in your organisation would need to have taken place to have reached this point.

❑ Why pursue equality of opportunity?

Whatever the individual or organisational definition of equality of opportunity, there are a number of reasons, both ethical and pragmatic, compelling schools and colleges to work to achieve it. Firstly the law demands it, and employees' recourse to industrial tribunals has become both more frequent and more successful in recent years. Such cases, though rare, are both very expensive and embarrassing for the organisation. Also emphasising the pragmatic approach, in some areas of education a predicted shortage of labour will mean organisations need to work hard at retention and attraction:

> At a time of labour shortages equal opportunities becomes more a matter of self-interest for the employer than one of altruism (Wagstaff, 1994, p. 102).

Beyond fear of prosecution and self-interest, there is a relationship between the learning of students and equality of opportunity for staff. Men and women in schools and colleges act as role models, and, for example, as Marshall (1994, p. 3) points out, it is no good telling girls they can become doctors or astronauts if:

they can see in their schools that women who break sex-role stereotypes encounter barriers, lack of support, and marginalization.

Similarly, if minority ethnic children are encouraged to raise their aspirations but, as Clay, Cole and George report:

> Many believe that minority teachers get a raw deal – and (that) pupils know it (Clay, Cole and George, 1995, p. 22)

the hidden curriculum will powerfully undermine the relatively weak force of the intended curriculum. The involvement of a diverse staff is also likely to ensure that the knowledge and experience from which the curriculum is managed does not rest too uniformly on that of white, middle-class, able-bodied men.

Finally, there is growing evidence that the overall management of a school or college may benefit from the different strengths of both women and men (Hall, 1996; Coleman, 1996) and from those of different ethnic groups (Davidson, 1997).

❏ The current position

There is not space to present a full range of supporting statistics, but even a cursory glance at the figures collected by the Department for Education and Employment (DfEE) will show that women in the UK are under-represented at senior level in all phases of education and are paid less than men (DfEE, 1995). The higher the status of the institution, the more this is apparent, with, for example, only 5.5 per cent of professors in universities being women (AUT, 1995). Coleman's chapter, 'Women in educational management' in *The Principles of Educational Management* offers a more detailed picture of the current situation. Figures from outside the UK demonstrate a similar level of under-representation (Rujis, 1993). Women employed in education are often assigned particular roles considered appropriate to their gender, take longer to achieve promotion (Coleman, n.d.) and feel impelled to cultivate what Hall (1996) calls 'a perfect front'.

In the developing world, Freeman (1993, p. 12) reported that women in education:

> work longer hours than men, and have little, if any, free time. They have the additional burden of lack of adequate food/calories.

Despite optimism that progress has been made, women in education world-wide are disadvantaged compared to men.

The representation of minority ethnic staff in the UK is difficult to evidence, given that no national figures are collected for staff in schools and colleges, but the Swann Report (DES, 1985), the Commission for Racial Equality survey (1988) and the tiny number entering teacher training indicate the persistent degree of under-representation (Clay, Cole and George, 1995). Once employed, they are likely to be treated in different ways to majority ethnic staff:

> In many ways our presence within the education system acts as a buffer: we are used in a conciliatory fashion to contain dissatisfaction and diffuse potentially volatile situations, with black pupils and parents. Black teachers are often called upon to fill pastoral and disciplinary roles in situations where they have little control and are usually asked to intervene on behalf of the school rather than in the interests of black pupils or parents. A school can deflect allegations of racism by using its black staff to deal with situations or tensions, and even by citing their existence as proof of its commitment to challenging racism (Bangar and McDermott, 1989, p. 141).

Further examples could be given of other forms of discrimination, the grim experience of homosexuals (Vosper and Smith, 1993), the attribution of certain stereotypical characteristics to those who teach in certain subject areas, the failure to reach the UK suggested target of 3 per cent of disabled employees, but even this brief snapshot evidences the fact that schools and colleges are still far from places where the existence of equality of opportunity can be assumed.

❏ The causes of inequality

Understanding the theory of the causes of inequality may be a support for managers attempting to achieve their own vision of equal opportunity. However:

> The politics of race and gender is characterised by a diversity of perspectives and profound disagreement about what the problems are, their causes and solutions. Indeed, what defines the new politics of race and gender is dissatisfaction with conventional liberal solutions, and the search for new policy alternatives, and the ensuing dissension over ends and means (Marshall, 1994, p. 1).

The dominance of the liberal approach in this area, avoiding radical change, may be partly because other approaches may be perceived as more threatening and therefore provoke more resistance, but also because, however unsatisfactory, it does offer an agenda for action. Positive action training for women, minorities and those with disabilities, anti-discriminatory training for those appointing staff, and monitoring against criteria of statistical representation is at least a practical agenda. Theorists who espouse alternative approaches would suggest that the 'progress' achieved by these means is in fact no such thing, simply a perpetuation of the previous norms, and to truly achieve progress, a different and more profound understanding of the causes of inequality is needed. Theory falls into three broad categories:

1. Economic theories – suggest that the position of women and minorities relate to their role in the economy. Women are primarily needed for their reproductive, rather than productive role, and will consequently be less valuable in the workplace. Similarly, minority ethnic people are perceived as an additional workforce to be used in areas not attractive to the majority ethnic population. The position of any individual remains subordinate until their economic value equals that of the dominant group.

2. Radical theories – suggest that women and minorities are oppressed, and that even were they to undertake a representative proportion of jobs at senior level or in areas from which they have been traditionally absent, they would still be valued less. The reproducers of oppression are fundamentals such as the use of space, language and sexual relations.

3. Class, race and gender related theories – suggest that no one cause of discrimination or oppression can be seen in isolation from the others. As Freeman (1993) points out, where gender acts as a bar to the majority of Indian women in many areas, if the class of the woman is high enough, the bar is overruled. Similarly, a white women teacher may stand in a dominant power relation to a black, male teacher (Liddle and Joshie, 1987).

The understanding of the causes of inequality will influence how the individual manager plans to remedy the situation. A radical theorist would see little point in striving to encourage women senior managers if the style of management, including the use of language and relationships with other staff, were not congruent with the predilections of the women concerned. A manager with a race, class and gender perspective would see the growth of numbers of white women in senior positions, while black staff were still confined to junior positions, as a regressive step, simply reinforcing the dominance of the majority ethnic group. The choice of means to achieve progress relates to the theoretical understanding of the cause. The only certainty is that the widely used, liberal equal opportunities approach has failed to achieve the equal representation of women and minority ethnic people to which it aspires. Consequently, managers may need to progress further in their thinking and their action, despite the fact that alternative theories offer no single and obvious agenda for action.

Activity

How would you characterise the discourse on equal opportunities in your organisation? List the actions which your organisation has taken to promote equality of opportunity. Which theoretical frameworks appear to underpin them? Has the organisation moved beyond the traditional liberal approach?

❑ Taking action

The experience of teachers and associate staff in the system is that a real, rather than a rhetorical, commitment to equal opportunity would demand that issues are addressed in an holistic and consistent fashion over time. The one-off drive or project is unlikely to have any effect:

> It is so often assumed that fighting racism involves taking a few decisions, making a few concessions and then ticking anti-racism off the list as a job well done. The ingenuity and versatility of the racist system in subverting each new measure employed to counter its racism is rarely understood (Bangar and McDermott, 1989, p. 149).

Equality of opportunity for students relates to equality for staff, as the hidden messages are inevitably part of learning. Changing the culture of an organisation to one in which no assumptions are made about people on the basis of their gender, race or class, disability or any other irrelevant factor will, as with any culture change, require long-term effort and consistent support from those in power. The difficulty in the area of equal opportunity, as Freeman (1993) points out, is that it cannot be taken for granted that those in power will be motivated to work towards a situation in which their own power and preferred norms may be threatened. Wagstaff (1994) asserts optimistically that:

> The combination of labour shortages, major shifts in employment legislation and some move in values should lead to the employment of a workforce more representative of the whole population (Wagstaff, 1994, p. 102).

As has been discussed, this may not be viewed by some as a great triumph. The experience of black men and women who have achieved senior positions is that they still suffer under a burden of disadvantage (Osler, 1997). The argument that greater numbers of women, black or disabled people in the system, particularly at senior levels, will eventually bring about culture change may convince you. If on the other hand, you feel that those succeeding are likely to do so by adopting wholly, or in part, the norms and behaviour of the dominant group, or to be distracted by opposition to such, a sustained determination to change not only the demography of people in schools and colleges but also the values and culture of all will be needed if equality of opportunity is to be achieved.

❑ Building on key learning points

- Equal opportunities is a concept with universal support at the general level, but at the operational level of defining goals and the practical action to achieve them, is very contested.

- Theories analysing the underlying causes of inequality offer very different interpretations of the goals and the means to achieve them.

- The liberal approach has dominated to date, but in its own terms of achieving representative numbers of 'disadvantaged' groups within every organisation, has failed to achieve its aim.

- More radical and holistic solutions may be required, but this will entail a political approach which seeks to enrol all, particularly those with power, in long-term cultural change.

 Reading

*Marianne Coleman's chapter, 'Managing for equal opportunities: the gender issue' in **Managing People in Education**, offers a detailed consideration of the causes of inequality amongst men and women in education and reviews individual, organisational and national strategies to address inequality.*

Managing stress

This section considers:

- the rising concern at stress in education
- definitions of stress
- the causes of stress
- remedies to reduce stress
- time management.

❏ Concern at the effects of stress in education

The management of stress has become an issue of urgency in many schools and colleges. Managers have recognised that a degree of stress is required to achieve optimum performance, but that too much stress can result in a range of psychological, physiological and behavioural symptoms which may have a negative effect on the individual member of staff, the organisation and ultimately the pupils/students. Put simply, the consequence of stress which is out of control may be people who:

> cannot cope with the demands of their job and their willingness to try drops dramatically (Travers and Cooper, 1996, p. 24).

The impact on the individual may be health problems which span a minor to life-threatening spectrum. The impact on the organisation may include high absenteeism, high labour turnover, rising health-related early retirement, industrial relations difficulties and, of course, impaired teaching and learning (Travers and Cooper, 1996). A survey of further education staff found very high levels of stress (see Figure 5.1).

The concern is shared world-wide. In Western Australia (Punch and Tuettmann, 1990), Hong Kong (Chan and Hui, 1995), New Zealand (Galloway *et al.*, 1986) and many other countries, surveys have identified the negative impact of symptoms of high stress levels amongst those working in education.

Within Europe there is a legal obligation for the employer to provide a safe environment (EU, 1989) including taking reasonable steps to avoid exposing employees to pressures which may damage health. Much more exigent is the belief that unless stress is controlled, the damage to individuals and to learning in schools and colleges will be increasingly destructive.

❏ Defining stress

Those who seek to understand stress better as a foundation for their personal or organisational response are hampered by the absence of agreement on exactly what stress is. A myriad studies have failed to reach consensus. A useful framework for distinguishing three different approaches to understanding stress is given by Rees (1989):

1. The **engineering model** describes stress as pressure exerted on an individual by the environment . . . Pressure that is excessive or too frequently applied, takes the individual beyond the limits of his

	Never %	On a few occasions only	Some of the time	Most of the time	All the time	Number
All staff	0	8.8	49.9	35.8	5.5	385
Full-time staff	0	7.6	47.3	38.7	6.3	315

Figure 5.1   The degree to which 'stress at work' is felt (Earley, 1994, p. 9)

or her flexibility and results in a break or permanent damage . . . the state of permanent damage caused by prolonged or repeated stress is often described as 'burnout'.

2. **The physiological model** . . . which concentrates on the manifestations of stress in the individual (i.e. loss of sleep, increased heart rate, etc.).

3. Definitions which focus on the discrepancy between demands and ability have been described as **transactional models**.

(Adapted from Rees, 1989, pp. 6–7.)

Travers and Cooper (1996) simplify the concept of stress further by describing **stress as a response** to some factor in the environment, **stress as a stimulus**, that is the factors or 'stressors' in the environment which provoke a response, and **stress as an interaction**, a complex process involving synthesis of both of the previous concepts. Most now agree that focusing on just the individual response or just the environment causing stress may not be helpful. The interaction concept may help explain why individuals experience different stress levels when faced with the same level of pressure, and consequently may help those faced with managing stress.

❑ The causes of stress

Much of the thrust of research to date has been concerned with understanding why individuals experience stress differently, with attempts to find a correlation between personality traits, gender, age, types of school/college, organisational factors and stress levels. No such correlation has been definitively identified. Analysis can focus on the factors in society, in the organisation and in the individual. There is no doubt that there is a general belief that society has generally become more stressful, with longer work hours and an increased pace of change. From the perspective of the organisation, several researchers provide lists of possible stressors. An example is Rees (1989) who includes amongst stressors:

- pupil attitude and behaviour
- poor career prospects
- poor physical environment
- constraints on resources
- excessive workload and time pressures
- poor organisation and management within the school
- conflict in relationships
- pace of change
- interface between work and home.

A further dimension may be understanding the impact of stress over time as integral to the role of the teacher and to other professions which deal with people, such as the police and health services. As Kyriacou (1987) points out, it is not the unique highly stressful event which may lead to breakdown, but the:

insidious day-to-day sources of stress with their cumulative effect . . . the general level of alertness and vigilance required by teachers in meeting the potentially threatening variety of demands made upon them that constitutes the essence of why the experience of stress and burnout is so prevalent (Kyriacou, 1987, p. 148).

Specific roles have also been identified as a potential source of stress, with middle managers particularly at risk due to the ubiquitousness of role conflict and role ambiguity (Doring, 1993).

The relationship between personality and stress has also been studied. However, the fact that teachers are a self-selecting group and that those studied are the survivors have undermined attempts to draw strong connections. Type A personalities have been suggested as being particularly vulnerable to stress. Travers and Cooper suggest that we would recognise type A teachers by the fact that they:

- work long hours constantly under deadlines and conditions of overload

- take work home on evenings and at weekends; they are unable to relax
- often cut holidays short to get back to work, or may not even take a holiday
- constantly compete with themselves and others; also drive themselves to meet high, often unrealistic standards
- feel frustrated in the work situation
- are irritable with work efforts and their pupils
- feel misunderstood by their headteachers (Travers and Cooper, 1996, p. 68).

This personality type is one of the two major areas of exploration in relation to stress and personality. The second is the impact of belief as to where the 'locus of control' resides. Put simply, those who believe they have control over their lives, that the locus of control is with them as individuals, may be more resistant to stress than those who believe that they have little control and that the locus of control is external to them (Kyriacou, 1987). The belief in ability to control one's life may be one of the factors resulting in 'hardiness' (Pierce and Molloy, 1990), that is a resistance to stressors. Although exploration of these two factors is the most prevalent in research to date, there are many analyses of other traits. It is not possible to define which traits make it likely that individuals will experience stress, but it may be possible to be forewarned that personality traits may inflate the degree of stress experienced:

> As regards the question of personality variables, therefore, it is not possible to say that particular traits will lead to stress although they have been identified as associated with it. A more convincing hypothesis is that there may be a 'vicious circle' of interaction between stress and certain personality traits, with one tending to exaggerate the other (Rees, 1989, p. 19)

❑ Alleviating stress

Attempts to minimise stress overload have approached the problem from two angles: what the individual can do and what the organisation can do. Rees (1989) identifies two types of coping pattern open to the individual:

> direct action (by which the individual attempts to reduce the perceived threat by reducing the demands on him or herself); and palliative action (by which the individual attempts to moderate his or her perception of threat or emotional response to demands) (Rees, 1989, p. 8).

Palliative action is often most difficult when help is most needed. The more stressed a member of staff may be, the harder it becomes for him or her to adjust attitude and response. In extreme cases, only when ill health results in a period of absence does the individual have a release of pressure which allows them to rethink their position. Such rethinking is possible but difficult when remaining subject to the sources of stress. Direct action can also be problematic. Workshops sometimes focus on staff removing some pressure by 'saying no' or cutting down the work they do. However, reducing the work level can bring its own penalties and pressures:

> Even if you say to yourself, 'Well I'm not going to do it this weekend, I'm not going to work, I'm not going to prepare that,' you seem to pay a price for it later because you are disorganised or you can't do something you want to do because you haven't got the materials together and you haven't thought it out properly (Cockburn, 1994, p. 383).

Similarly, withdrawal from particularly stressful situations may reduce the pressure, but also removes contact with the support of colleagues and the satisfaction and pride of working with students:

> Some individuals try to cope by withdrawal from situations which are seen as stressful, although this seems to be an unsuccessful long-term coping strategy for the individual . . . One reason for this may be that the teacher who withdraws from potential demands of pupils is also withdrawing from potential sources of satisfaction and reward, while withdrawal from relationships with colleagues precludes the possibility of social support (Rees, 1989, p. 4).

This is not to say that direct and palliative action are of no use to the individual, but it does suggest that simplistic approaches which depend on the action of the individual alone may be limited in success.

Types of action which can be undertaken by the organisation are defined by Rees (1989) in a similar way to that of individuals:

> Mirroring the distinction between direct and palliative coping techniques is the distinction between 'instrumental' and 'emotional' support. In the former category come various aspects of organisational and career structure; in the latter, such actions as the development of 'pastoral care' for staff to support the formation of good relationships (Rees, 1989, p. 46).

The response of the individual to stress is likely to be complex, culturally sensitive (Gaziel, 1993) and related to factors both within and outside work. If the organisation is to keep stress at a level where it is likely to enthuse and invigorate staff, then Travers and Cooper (1996) argue that the response of managers must be a 'multi-dimensional approach to teacher stress alleviation' (p. 157). They offer a list of possible stress management interventions suggested by teachers. Not all of the actions suggested will be open to every organisation, but some will be possible. A whole organisation approach which attempts to operate a variety of palliative and direct actions at individual and organisational level may be a way of halting the epidemic of stress overload.

 Reading

*Megan Crawford's chapter, 'Managing stress in education', in **Managing People in Education**, explores the range of strategies which individuals and organisations can take to manage stress. She offers many further ideas on how managers can tackle inappropriate levels of stress, whether too much or too little.*

❏ Managing time

Time management is often seen as a subset of managing stress, as work overload appears frequently in studies on the causes of stress. Workload appears to have increased considerably. A survey of further education staff confirmed this trend, though self-reported figures must be treated with some caution (see Figure 5.2).

Jim Campbell and Sean St J. Neill's chapter on managing teachers' time in *Managing People in Education* offers some useful insights into how the way teachers spend their time has changed in the last two decades.

Both individuals and organisations have taken action to try to manage their time better (Cockburn, 1994; Blanchard *et al.*, 1990). Books and courses continue to offer ideas. 'Time Management' techniques usually centre around a number of themes:

- **Time planning**
  Identifying prime objectives
  Listing and prioritising tasks
  Allocating blocks of time
  Eliminating prevarication and butterflying from job to job
  Keeping a diary and reviewing how time is actually used against planned use

Workload has increased by	%	N
About a tenth	15.8	49
About a quarter	37.7	117
About a third	24.5	76
About a half	11.9	37
About three-quarters	2.3	7
About double	5.5	17
More than double	2.3	7

Figure 5.2   The extent of increase in workload (Earley, 1994, p. 7)

- **Controlling personal contacts**
  Finding ways of signalling availability and non-availability
  Preventing interruptions
  Controlling telephone calls

- **Delegation**
  Using staff, both associate and teaching, to undertake tasks which it is appropriate to delegate
  Getting the best out of administrative support

- **Managing meetings**
  Ensuring the purpose and intended outcomes of meetings are clear
  Eliminating unhelpful diversions
  Ensuring follow up to ensure time spent in meetings is productive

However:

time management is a potentially dangerous concept in practice. Faced with absurdly demanding expectations, class teachers who do not meet them all effectively should not be made to feel that the reason for not meeting them is their failure to manage their own time properly. This would be to blame the victim (Campbell, 1992, p. 27).

There comes a point when no amount of time management will help individuals achieve what is simply too much work. Equally, teachers' capacity to manage their time may be very impaired by the nature of teaching:

In teaching there are a lot of what we call 'time bandits'. No matter how well you prepare, how well organised you are, things happen during the course of the day that you haven't planned for, that eat into your time (Cockburn, 1994, p. 377).

The combined effect of too great demands and the interrupted nature of work may explain the almost universal experience of crisis management as the norm (Earley and Fletcher-Campbell, 1992). Time management courses may not have the desired effect, as such techniques as the ability to prioritise, order and delegate work may result in the perceived capacity for more work to be loaded on:

I told him I had even taken a seminar on time management. Frankly, I think the course made things worse. In the first place, attending it got me two days further behind in my work. Moreover, even though it helped me become a bit more efficient, I think my increased efficiency merely made room for more work because no matter how much I did there was always more to do (Blanchard *et al.*, 1990, p. 21).

There is no easy answer to reducing work overload and creating time. Superficial palliative techniques may bring short-term relief, but for long-term benefit, a culture change, relating to perceptions and expectations, is required. If an individual's ability to handle over-large workloads, willingness to limit time with the family, willingness to take on all the 'extras' are met with approval, admiration and even promotion, those who resist such a pattern will be penalised. Senge (1990) argues that individuals and organisations should explore if demands are self or organisation imposed and find leverage for cultural change at both levels, because unless time is created, there is no possibility of achieving a learning organisation, and stress levels may become intolerable.

Activity

Reflect on the attitudes towards workloads and time management in your organisation. How would you characterise the culture? How are those who work very long hours viewed? How would someone who did not take work home and who worked the contractual hours only be viewed? Canvass the views of colleagues.

❏ Comment

Your own views and those of colleagues will indicate to you the current culture and how far attitudes are likely to promote a sustainable level of work. You may have found that those in senior positions feel impelled to set an example of working harder or longer hours than others, or that they attempt to set a standard of a reasonable balance of work with other commitments and activities. Resisting a culture of 'incessant busyness' (Senge, 1990, p. 305) may provoke an unfavourable response and even criticisms concerning level of commitment, but without such culture change Senge argues that a learning organisation will not be achieved and stress levels may become detrimental to the individual and the organisation.

❏ Building on key learning points

- There is no universally agreed definition of what stress is, but the current consensus amongst researchers seems to be that the notion of an interaction between an individual and the environment is the most fruitful basis for understanding stress and planning to manage it.

- Research into the causes of stress in the individual and in the school or college environment have led to a myriad and sometimes contradictory conclusions.

- Personality traits do have an effect on any individual's experience of stress and their ability to manage it, but any simple equation of stress level with particular traits is not possible.

- Action can be direct or palliative, and taken at individual and/or organisational level. A multi-dimensional long-term approach is most likely to be of real help to staff.

- More effective time management will not deal with issues of overload. The nature of teaching means that time will always appear insufficient. Individual time management techniques may be helpful, but in the long term, rewarding and praising those who control their workload, rather than admiring those who cope with unreasonable loads, may begin to undermine the universal expectation that those in education work over-long hours.

Managing motivation

This section considers:

- the importance of motivation
- theories of motivation
- approaches to motivating staff.

The purpose of an organisation is to enable ordinary human beings to do extraordinary things. No organisation can depend on genius; the supply is always scarce and unreliable. It is the test of an organisation to make ordinary people perform better than they seem capable of (Drucker, 1989, p. 155).

Drucker's quotation neatly encapsulates the foundation of a manager's effectiveness, the ability to ensure that all the people with whom he or she works fulfil their potential, achieving a performance which delights themselves and the organisation. The capacity to achieve such performance levels is bound up with the concept of **motivation**, relating to individual behaviour, and **morale**, relating to the general motivation amongst a group of people. Managers search for ways of ensuring that staff want to stay in the organisation and want to achieve in a way which is aligned to the organisation's objectives. There are a host of theories analysing the possible correlation between motivation and performance, aimed at providing a basis for the manager to influence the strength and direction of staff actions.

A simple start point of belief that improving the nature of a job role and the conditions of work will increase motivation cannot be assumed. Staff can be highly motivated even when working in conditions of great adversity and sometimes because of the adversity. Mwamwenda (1995) concludes that, in keeping with surveys in Canada, Japan, Singapore, Germany and Albania, the majority of teachers in his sample in South Africa, despite extremely difficult conditions, are satisfied with their job and still consider teaching 'a fine and challenging profession'. Any simple equation which assumes that motivation decreases in ratio to poor conditions or increased adversity does not take account of the human spirit. Theorists may disagree on much, but the fact that motivation is a complex and individual process is not in dispute.

❑ Major theories of motivation

Managers in education have sought to understand motivation and the degree to which they can influence it. As Turner summarises:

> The question is not whether staff are motivated, but whether anything the manager does will make any difference (Turner, 1992, p. 8).

To answer this question a sophisticated understanding is needed, synthesising the work of theorists to date. One of the earliest and best known theorists was Maslow (1943), who argued that motivation related to meeting a hierarchy of needs (see Figure 5.3).

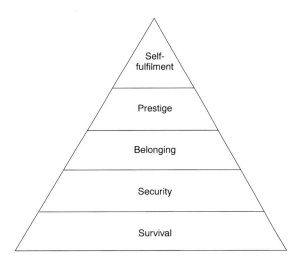

Figure 5.3   Maslow's hierarchy of needs

The most important aspect of his theory is that satisfaction of needs is sequential, and, for example, that people will not be motivated by self-actualisation needs when lower levels are unmet. The absolute nature of this theory ignores individual response, and though there may be some value for managers in recognising the different range of needs, the belief that needs are met in strict hierarchical order is discredited.

As outlined in more detail in Colin Riches' chapter on motivation in *The Principles of Educational Management*, McGregor (1970) built on Maslow's ideas by suggesting that there were two ways of viewing the motivation of people, the 'X' and 'Y' theory. Theory 'X' suggests that people generally seek to avoid work and must be pressured by managers and/or driven by the need to make a living. Theory 'Y' views people as wanting to take responsibility for themselves and be self-directed. Theory 'X' and 'Y' can be a useful means of analysing the underlying assumptions about the way people behave implicit in any policy or approach.

Herzberg (1966) approached motivation differently, suggesting that managers must work in two ways, to make staff positively satisfied and to remove the factors which dissatisfy. Although this may seem obvious, the important addition to theory was Herzberg's belief that the effects of these two were independent.

Herzberg drew some important conclusions:

(1) The things which make people happy at work are not simply the opposites of the things which make them unhappy, and vice versa. The two sets of things are different in kind. You will not make people satisfied, therefore, simply by removing the causes of dissatisfaction.

(2) The things that make people dissatisfied are related to the job environment. The things that make people satisfied, on the other hand, are related to job content.

(3) While those who have a satisfying job may have a higher tolerance of dissatisfiers, the dissatisfying factors can be so strong that the job becomes intolerable.

(4) Managers must therefore be concerned with ensuring both that the causes of dissatisfaction are removed and that opportunities for satisfaction are increased – that, in Herzberg's terms, the job is 'enriched' (Everard and Morris, 1990, p. 29).

This dual approach has proved both helpful and confusing for managers. The conflation of the concepts of motivation and satisfaction have led to flawed assumptions:

- that staff who are satisfied must be motivated
- that staff who are satisfied work harder
- that measures of satisfaction equate to measures of motivation.

In fact satisfaction and motivation are quite different. Motivation describes the impetus to take action, the direction and persistence of the action (Turner, 1992). Satisfaction is:

a function of the gap between the rewards actually granted and the rewards an individual thinks he/she deserves (Kremer-Hayon and Goldstein, 1990, p. 287).

Consequently Herzberg's use of the terms 'satisfier' and 'dissatisfier' has perhaps proved more confusing than helpful.

Both of these theories focus on motivation as action to meet needs. Other theories approach the concept from the angle of understanding how people decode the probable results of their action, and whether this encourages them to instigate or continue particular behaviour. **Expectancy theory** (Handy, 1993) assumes that each individual makes a personal calculation of the costs and benefits of choices of action, and responds accordingly. The advantage of this theory is that it encompasses the very personal nature of motivation.

Related to this is **goal theory**, which argues that people will be motivated by a goal which they see as stretching them to the degree they wish and in a direction they endorse. The important factors for managers using this theory is that goals should be agreed and at a level which is appropriate to the individual. McClelland (1961) studied the relationship of goals and motivation. He estimated that about 10 per cent of the population have a highly developed motivation to achieve, but as this is likely to be found more in managers and in the professions, it is likely to be present in a much higher percentage of staff in education. He identified certain characteristics of high achievers:

1. Achievers like to set their own goals, and are quite selective about the goals they adopt, and so are unlikely to automatically accept the goals suggested by others, including their managers. They prefer to be fully responsible for their own success or failure, and only seek help from experts or those who can provide useful information.

2. They tend to choose moderate goals, avoiding those which are very difficult or easy. The goal which stretches will be chosen, but not one where gaining it is doubtful or a matter of luck.

3. The achiever prefers tasks which provide more or less immediate feedback.

(Adapted from Everard and Morris, 1990, pp. 33–4).

The high percentage of people with such characteristics in the professions, and in education specifically, may go some way towards explaining why the motivation and management of staff cannot replicate that in industry and business, but must take account of the parameters that are likely in influencing people's performance.

Finally, **equity** or **exchange theory** suggests that people will be motivated by a sense of fair play, and that perceptions of being treated less favourably than others will demotivate.

Much of this writing is based on research which took place in America quite a while ago, and which may not have adequately addressed issues of gender, race and culture. Hofstede's (1980) research showed that the sort of leadership which empowers and which has been interpreted as leading to motivation in the West (Peters, 1989) is not always perceived as appropriate or motivating in other cultures. Theory provides a range of ideas which may be helpful, but cannot substitute for approaching motivation through an understanding of the individual, and the organisational context within which he or she works.

❑ Motivating staff

Managers can seek to influence the factors which impact on motivation at different levels:

N.C.I LIBRARY

Variables affecting motivation can be found at three levels in organisational settings:

- variables unique to the individual (e.g. attitudes, interests, specific needs),
- variables which arise from the nature of the job (e.g. degree of control over the job, level of responsibility), and
- variables related to the organisational environment (e.g. peer group relations, supervisory practices, system-wide rewards and organisational climate) (Vandevelde, 1988, p. 12).

At the level of the individual, the intrinsic motivation to enjoy relations with pupils and colleagues, to pursue specific interests and to feel competent and of worth can be promoted. The actual job can be shaped in ways which are likely to increase motivation. The degree of clarity/ambiguity, autonomy/ direction, and the nature of goals can be moulded to the individual as far as is practicable within organisational objectives. At organisational level, the reward systems can be made transparent and as far as possible equitable, the physical environment improved, and social cohesion enabled through structures to promote communication. Some actions may not be available. For example, pay may be determined, the buildings old and unattractive, but though all measures may not be possible, a good range will. In a survey of 3,019 teachers, the factors seen as very important in safeguarding their own personal motivation were:

- job satisfaction
- good relations with pupils
- being able to give pupils a sense of achievement
- having sufficient time for family and private life
- well-managed school
- good school discipline (Vaarlem, Nuttall and Walker, 1992, p. ii).

Actions to promote these general conditions are open to all.

If motivation is to be predicated on understanding individuals, it is also clear that the responsibility must lie with sufficient people to enable them to relate to a small enough group of people to allow a personal strategy to motivate the individual to be evolved. This has implications for the line management structure, and for the role delineation and training of managers throughout the organisation. The organisation can put in place a number of activities and structures likely to increase motivation, but this cannot replace an approach which recognises the complexity of motivation in each unique individual, and which avoids a homogeneous approach to human motivation.

Activity

You may wish to reflect on your own motivation over time. Have the same things motivated you throughout your career or have different factors come to the fore at different times? Have those who have managed you motivated you and if so how? Are there common patterns or have different strategies proved successful as your career developed?

❑ **Building on key learning points**

- Motivating people is one of the keystones of achieving a successful organisation.

- Researchers on motivation offer no one comprehensive theory, but do suggest that although motivation is a complex individual phenomenon, there are a variety of actions which are likely to increase motivation and remove the barriers which inhibit motivation.

- Any plan to motivate staff will need to take account of the complexity of each individual's response.

 Reading

Colin Riches' chapter, 'Motivation', in **The Principles of Educational Management,** *offers a more extensive explanation and critique of the main theories of motivation. It also suggests a model of motivation where the mental and physical health of the individual may override any other motivating factors to the detriment of performance. In this way a clear link is drawn between managing stress and motivation.*

Developing a team(s)-based approach

This section considers:

- possible criteria for teams' effectiveness
- types of teams
- team development and leadership factors.

Teams for various reasons have increasingly become attractive to managers as a means of organising organisational work to achieve organisational objectives. Coleman and Bush (1994, p. 266) suggest this attraction is 'because they encourage the participation of teachers in decision-making, leading to a sense of ownership and an enhanced prospect of successful innovation. One of the main features of collegiality is its emphasis on teamwork.' Some of the specific reasons, based on advocates of teams such as Peters (1987) and Handy (1993), are:

- Teams are more suitable to represent the range of interests in an organisation than is any individual.
- Teams are likely to produce more creative solutions than an individual, because of the pooling and harnessing of several talents.
- Team members are more likely to understand and support decisions made by 'their' teams.
- Team membership improves communication among members.
- Team membership can offer valuable opportunities for personal and professional development.

Widespread use of teams is as evident in schools and colleges as it is in other organisations, but the effective manager needs to be aware also of the possible limitations of what a team approach can achieve.

Firstly, there is the challenge to the *assumption* that teams must inevitably be better than individuals, graphically described by Sinclair (1992) as 'the tyranny of team ideology'. Leithwood (1996, p. 21) adds that 'relatively little is known about the processes through which teams actually learn to accomplish their tasks'.

Secondly, O'Neill (1994b, 1997) and Little (1990) have been among those pointing out that the core activity of staff (i.e. teaching) in schools and colleges is essentially a 'private', largely autonomous and individualistic one and that therefore the notion of teamwork with its demands for openness and commitment to peers may be threatening or at least uncomfortable to individuals.

Thirdly, it can be agreed that there exists a lack of accountability for the performance of teams. Appraisal in schools and colleges concentrates mostly upon individuals and/or the whole organisation. Arrangements begun in 1998 in England and Wales that the performance of governing bodies of schools be included (and graded) in the inspection of schools provide an interesting exception to this since it is the governing *body* (or team?) alone, not individual governors, who are inspected and assessed.

Finally, and linked with the previous point, is that the notion of establishing effectiveness criteria for team performance is not widespread either in theory or in practice in education.

 Reading

*John O'Neill's chapter, 'Managing through teams', in **Managing People in Education**, discusses the question of whether teams are 'natural' for teachers and argues that conflict needs to be seen as inevitable and positive if such teams are to be effective.*

❏ Team effectiveness

If the manager's commitment to a team approach is to be based on more than theory – or wish-fulfilment – it needs to include a clear idea of what constitutes an *effective* team. Katzenbach and Smith (1993) argue that introducing team approaches will be meaningless 'unless the organisation has a robust performance ethic' (p. 24). Essentially, the team members have to be convinced that performance truly matters, otherwise teams could at worst become a shelter for excuses for weak performance.

With this in mind, and linked with the work of Leithwood (1996), we suggest a workable set of **criteria for team effectiveness** might be:

1. the extent to which the quantity and quality of specified outcomes for the team has been achieved

2. the extent to which the working of the team has enhanced its future capacity as a team

3. the extent to which the capacity of individual team members has been enhanced.

❏ Types of teams in schools and colleges

The rational or bureaucratic perspective of Scott (1987) that a team is a group of three or more people pursuing a specific set of goals within the context of a formalised set of structures is not tenable in 'open systems' organisations which schools and colleges have become. Particularly, the enormously increased interaction with parents and the community means that goals and interests of these organisations shift, are regularly negotiable and are usually influenced by environmental factors.

We suggest that broadly there are three different types of teams in schools and colleges:

(a) **The statutory team**: these bodies are *required* to exist as groups and must therefore reach 'team' decisions. Governing bodies of schools and colleges in England and Wales, site councils in some US regions, community college councils, student councils are examples from various countries of such bodies. Membership and roles are usually clearly specified but ambiguity can remain around general purposes, specific goals and working procedures and the circumstances of the bodies do not 'lend themselves to the idea of a team' (Leithwood, 1996, p. 8). Two particular problems can be identified:

(i) Infrequency of meeting and communication militate against opportunity for team learning and individual development.

(ii) Membership by role is for a prescribed period for individuals filling that role so that the team's future capacity can rarely be developed.

(b) **The 'standing' team**: by this, we mean the teams which are established, membership through role, to co-ordinate the work either of peers (e.g. senior managers (SMT)), or middle managers (heads of faculties), or those teaching the same subject or the same students (e.g. primary curriculum subject teams, school or college departmental teams).

This is easily the largest category and the one which most readily springs to mind in thinking of teams in schools and colleges. Research on SMT (Wallace and Hall, 1994), on departmental leadership of teams (Earley and Fletcher-Campbell, 1992), and effective secondary school departments (Sammons, Thomas and Mortimore, 1997) have all focused on these teams, because they are the ones most directly concerned with the day-to-day activity of the organisation and therefore the delivery of its performance. Because membership of these teams is automatically via role or status, interest in the team's ability to perform and to develop its future capacity is considerable. In education, this focus and its relationship to team composition has led to interest in the examination of role typology, the best known example being that of Belbin (1981, 1993, p. 66).

◎ Reading and Activity

Please read pages 266–72 of the chapter 'Managing with teams' by Marianne Coleman and Tony Bush in **Principles of Educational Management.**

Analyse a team of which you are a member by applying Belbin's typology. How much correspondence to his model is there in your team? Do you think such an approach to team composition might be helpful?

(c) **The 'project' or 'task' team**: this is the team with a strictly defined goal, to be achieved within a defined period of time. Its goal, often related to solving a problem, is necessarily a whole school/college one, or at least a cross-sectional one. The issues addressed may be curricular, pastoral, or anything which affects students or staff as a whole (transport, communications, environment). Membership will tend to be based upon those with an 'interest' in the issue, although how individual members are 'selected' remains a key management concern. Should members be volunteers, a representative sample, e.g. of area, experience, or chosen by a leader for 'expertise'?

Roade School in Northamptonshire, pursuing an industrial model, devised the system of Quality Improvement Teams (QUITS). Those teams had an agreed set of rules, including a life-span of 3–4 months, membership open to anyone who shared the problem, but total membership not exceeding 12 (ideally 8), and a 'non-interested' facilitator. A key commitment was that the instigator of the QUIT *must* accept the recommendations of the team!

❑ Composition of teams

As the work of Belbin and other research mentioned above has shown, and probably for all of us experience of working with other people has also indicated strongly, the factors affecting the composition of an effective team are by no means all to do with technical ability. Clearly a team (as the organisation of which it is part) will succeed partly through the knowledge, abilities and skills of those who work in it ('technical' aspects) and also though the degree of commitment, motivation and effort with which they apply these attributes ('functional' aspects). The latter are clearly affected by the character and personality of the individual, as well as the culture and structure of the school or college.

While the technical aspects of a team member are relatively easily discerned and assessed (team members will have been selected to work in the school or college *primarily* because of technical competence, e.g. in teaching itself, or librarianship, etc.), the functional aspects are more complex. The latter involve judgements about how people will 'fit', or how A will get on with B, or whether A and B are motivated by different things, for example.

However, this difficulty is relevant to **criterion 3** mentioned above (p. 49). An effective team will be one which eventually (i.e. at full performance) has enabled individual team members to develop as individual professionals and learn from each other in the process, i.e. team learning.

Before discussing this aspect of team development, something vital for managers to address, we need to note one of the factors, often seen as one of the biggest obstacles to developing effective teams in schools and colleges. This is the contribution to schools and colleges of part-time staff in particular and more generally that of all those who work in schools and colleges who are not full-time, fully paid teachers and lecturers. How does this impact upon a team-based approach?

If meeting regularly, both formally and informally, developing an ethos of sharing based on sound relationships and learning to 'give and take' with colleagues is central to developing a team, the manager has to address the issue of integrating part-time staff as important; if not, the risk of an inner team (full-time staff) plus others (part-time staff) is considerable. Research assignments by students on the MBA in Educational Management at Leicester University have explored this issue in primary, secondary and further education situations. The findings have almost always indicated that part-time staff feel less valued, less considered in decision-making, and less socially accepted (unless they had previously been full-time). At the same time, they felt they were expected to do proportionately more work! There are exceptions such as Campion School, Bugbrooke, where conscious decisions had been taken to integrate part-time staff such as ensuring they had permanent contracts and could apply for internal promoted posts.

As the possibility of individually negotiated contracts increases, MacFarlane (1998) suggests 'it is feasible to envisage a 1,000 pupil school with a core of full-time permanently employed teachers and a further 60 or so employed and supplied, either by an agency or a pool system run by the local authority' (p. 27). This situation is close to what already exists in further education colleges and provides the biggest threat to some of the assumptions about teams in schools and colleges.

While most teams in schools and colleges would consider it essential for associate staff to be automatically members of their teams (e.g. bursars in SMT, technicians in faculty teams), it is worth noting that 'project' teams may need to do much more. For example, a team examining a transport difficulty should surely include representatives(s) from the transport firm and a parent and any team exploring homework should probably have teachers and parents in equal measure.

❑ Team development

Because teams necessarily involve individual members joining together and bringing their personal characters and abilities to create the collective effort and performance of the team, it is obvious that team effectiveness does not emerge immediately. Each member learns as the team progresses, both about himself/herself and about other members; but there is also a 'team learning' process taking place.

Tuckman's model of team growth, devised in 1965 and described by O'Neill (1997) as 'remarkably enduring' (p. 80), suggests four main stages, described in mnemonic terms as:

> forming
> storming

norming

performing

It can be a useful exercise for team managers to reflect or systematically analyse at which stage the team members perceive the team is at any time. The model can be to managers a reassuring one by envisaging that ultimately performing teams are likely to go through a 'storming' stage. O'Neill himself argues that conflict between team members is not only inevitable in schools and colleges where the individual works mostly 'in private', but actually desirable and healthy. Since openness and candour in relationships and communications would seem to be a prerequisite for individuals eventually having conviction in and commitment to a common cause, this seems reasonable. What must surely bind people together, to enable that conflict not to be ultimately destructive, is what West-Burnham (1992) calls explicit and shared values. In schools and colleges these are certain to include certain professional values, including that the needs of the learning are paramount. The need for these values to be 'explicit' suggests an assumption that individuals *will* disagree.

Leithwood (1996) describes the process of team learning as 'mutual adaptation' (p. 13) and, although the phrase can have weak contextual implications (e.g. 'I will do less so she can do more!'), he claims that research indicates that 'multiple, mutual adaptations by team members, even of a quite conservative sort individually, have combined effects on a team's learning capable of producing radical changes in its collective mind and patterns of action' (p. 15).

❏ Team leadership

Leadership as a topic is fully explored in a parallel book in this series, *Leadership and Strategic Management*. However, it is clearly an important factor in team effectiveness. The value of work such as Belbin's, discussed earlier, is that it challenges the automatic assumption, for example, that Senior Role = Chair of Meeting = Team Leader. West-Burnham (1992) suggests that situational leadership is what is significant, i.e. where the person who has the abilities for a particular situation will lead in that situation and the leader by role's task is to facilitate. This is supported by Leithwood's (1996) model of Team Learning Processes, where the task of Team Leadership is to offer, for example, expert problem-solving processes, and practices which facilitate transformation rather than to be involved in the transactional processes of the team. With that in mind, Figure 5.4 can be offered as a summary which attempts to address the effectiveness criteria proposed earlier.

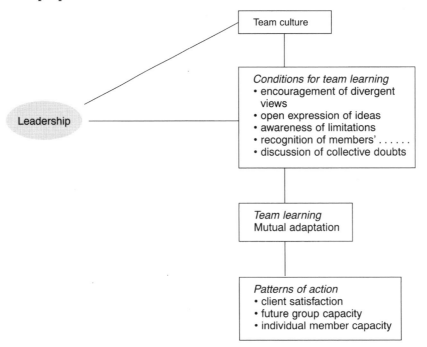

Figure 5.4   Team learning and action processes (based on Leithwood, 1996)

❑ **Building on key learning points**

- Teams should not be seen as a panacea for all staff issues.

- Clear criteria for assessing the effectiveness of teams are important.

- Different types of teams may be expected to operate and achieve in different ways.

- Managers need to be aware of what they expect in terms of the team learning and development.

Roles and structures

This section considers:

- the multiplicity of roles within educational organisations
- the significance of structures
- the relevance of structures to organisational change.

❑ Roles

In the previous section on teams, we have discussed roles which individuals may have in those teams. In the earlier section on stress, we also noted the potential harmful effects of role conflict. Of course, all those who work in a school or college undertake or are given specific roles the whole time. Individuals are appointed to fill a particular role (teacher, lecturer, librarian, bursar, site supervisor, etc.) but, just as team members may have both technical and functionalist roles, most people take on informal roles in their general work. Brain (1994, p. 97) suggests that in further education the lecturer is also 'learning facilitator/supporter, learning resource producer, information technology specialist, pastoral worker, marketeer, course/programme manager, deliverer of integrated core skills, raiser of European awareness, team worker, tester, assessor, examiner, deliverer of open/flexible/distance learning, administrator and increasingly manager.' These could all be seen as developments or extensions of the formal role. In addition, staff will inevitably take on various incidental or unofficial roles in the course of their daily work interacting with students and other staff. A group of headteachers of small primary schools listed among their roles those of electrician (replacing bulbs), goldfish feeders and guardians, toilet attendants, furniture removers and traffic controllers (TES, 1993)!

> **Activity**
>
> You may find it useful to list the various roles that *you* are called upon to fill during your time at work. Then, choose another staff member (e.g. member of office staff) and list their various roles. You may wish to check your second list out by actually asking that person. It is almost certain you will have missed some!

❑ Comment

This diversity of roles may be both threatening and exhausting on the one hand and exciting and fulfilling on the other. Valerie Hall in her chapter on 'Management roles' in *Managing People in Education* examines the complexity and growth of these roles in education but points out that 'It isn't all bad news' (p. 72). She makes a distinction between the role-*taker* and the opportunities that exist in the appropriate environment for individual staff to shape their roles (i.e. role-*makers*). The trend towards decentralised management provides that scope most significantly.

◎ Reading and Activity

Please read Valerie Hall's chapter.

What scope do you have in your current role for being a 'role-maker'? You may find it helpful to list those areas of your work where you must always refer to a line manager and those where you feel confident of taking your own initiative.

❑ Structures

The formal relationships between the official roles which are held by staff in schools and colleges are shown in the structure of the organisation. These structures are often depicted by charts which show the official pattern of the relationships, often placing a stress on who is accountable to whom. These charts are most usually shown as linear (see Figure 5.5).

Activity

If your college has such a chart (and schools will have similar ones), we suggest you examine it and assess its effectiveness in relation to what happens in most of your school or college's daily activities. Do communications, for example, always flow through the channels indicated on the chart? Is your own position accurately indicated?

You may also like to try to depict the structure in a concentric rather than linear way, by placing the key person at the centre of a circle and working outwards. Models that we have seen range from those placing the head/principal at the centre to those putting the students there!

❑ Purpose of structures

Whatever the particular form of structure, the manager needs to be clear what it is the structure is trying to achieve. Its overall function is clearly to achieve effectively and efficiently the organisation's key purpose. Given that, in schools and colleges, this key purpose is high quality learning, any criticism of a structure or proposal for restructuring should presumably ask the question: 'will/does this aid or improve learning?'

Other functions of structures (based on Mullins, 1989) may be:

- to enable the work of separate individuals and teams to be *monitored*
- to ensure the *accountability* of individuals and teams

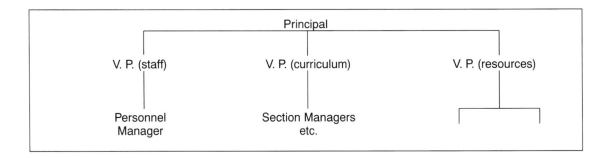

Figure 5.5   Example of an organisation structure chart

- to give staff *job satisfaction* and opportunity
- to be *flexible* enough to be adapted to changing circumstances, internal and external
- to enable *communications* and *decision-making* to be effective.

The list of emphasised words above may be seen as a set of criteria against which to assess the effectiveness of any school or college structure. If you use the criteria in analysing your own organisation's current structure, you will, of course, find that it is not perfect. The analysis may show, however, a weakness in one particular area.

Reading

Please read the chapter on 'Management structures' in* Managing People in Education. *Tony Bush suggests that integration is as important as differentiation for managers in developing structures. He also points out that salary issues in education have a powerful influence upon structures, so that flatter structures, for example, may lead to demotivation for some staff.

❑ Variations in structures

Although a set of functions may be agreed for structures in general, there will also be special 'determinants' which affect any particular school's or college's structure. Some of the determinants, may include:

- **size**, e.g. larger organisations tend to develop a network of interrelations between a number of different specialist groups

- **history**, e.g. the existence of highly paid senior staff may provide an obstacle to proposed restructuring because their abilities do not match new requirements

- **geographic dispersion**, e.g. split-site further education colleges and secondary schools may feel obliged to have more vice-principals or deputies because of the need to manage different sites

- **technology**, e.g. the growing influence of ICT may assume greater ease of communications.

Are there aspects of the current structure in your school or college which you believe exist because of special factors such as these?

❑ Structures and change

Changing the structures to influence how the organisation is intended to be managed is attractive to leaders and managers. A new headteacher or principal, for example, will often restructure in the early period of her/ his tenure in the attempt to improve effectiveness. Clearly, such changes are perceived to be helpful in improving practice. Those who believe in this mode of change are proposing that the order is firstly, get your structures right so that they support your educational goals, then get practice to conform to them. Werner (1991) argues that such structural changes are politically popular (for reasons such as the place needing a 'shake-up') but that they underestimate the traditions, assumptions and working relationships which profoundly shape existing practice. These traditions may be both positive and negative. As Hargreaves (1994, p. 351) points out, 'beliefs and practices are grounded not only in expertise and altruism, but also in structures in which considerable self-interest may be invested'. Change may therefore depend not only on releasing staff energy and ability but on controlling vested interests. Hargreaves suggests that sometimes it is necessary to make changes in structures to 'increase opportunities for meaningful working relationships and collegial support' (ibid., p. 351). For schools, he asserts that 'it is a challenge of redesigning school structures away from nineteenth and early twentieth-century models' (ibid., p. 351).

❑ Key learning points

- The diversity of roles may be exciting and threatening.

- Structures need to be assessed according to functions they are designed to fulfil.

- Reasons for structures need to be examined in relation to their capacity to help or hinder change.

Perhaps the most important issue for managers to realise about structures is that they are a means to an end and that restructuring therefore is not the end of any problems that may have existed but the *beginning* of an approach to their solution. The longer-term aim may be the establishment of a more appropriate culture, which will be discussed in the next section.

School and college cultures

This section considers:

- the recognition of cultures as an important factor in school/college management of HRM
- the features of culture in this context
- the capacity of managers to develop an appropriate culture.

❑ Importance of culture

Disaffection with rationalising approaches to business management paved the way for a series of books about management (notably *Corporate Cultures* by Deal and Kennedy, 1982 and *In Search of Excellence* by Peters and Waterman, 1982) which attempted to articulate a softer, people-oriented strategy for improving performance. The notion that successful companies (especially in the USA and Japan) had strong cohesive cultures, linked with the notion of schools and colleges needing to become more business-like, led to acceptance of the culture of educational organisations as being an important factor in their effective management. Similarly, Bush (1998) suggests that interest in culture 'may be explained, in part, as dissatisfaction with the limitations of the traditional, bureaucratic model' (p. 32).

Sergiovanni (1984) described schools as 'culturally tight and managerially loose' with the implication that influencing the culture will be at least as important as designing effective structures.

The large number of changes that schools and colleges have had to undergo in the late 1980s and in the 1990s have accentuated the emphasis on organisational culture because of the increased understanding of the complexity of change management in education. The increased awareness that real change only occurs through the extent of the staff's 'absorption' of the changes underlines the importance of those factors which constitute culture. Van Velzen and Robin (1985) argue that the reason that external or government demands were filtered and/or ignored by schools and colleges was that these organisations 'owned themselves' with separate and distinct cultures. Certainly, in the context of Total Quality Management and the consideration of its relevance to educational organisations, Atkinson (1990) says that organisations 'need to consider organisational culture and values as being *the* real issue for change in the 1990s' (Atkinson, 1990, p. 52).

❑ What is culture and its relevance to HRM?

Culture may most simply be defined in any single organisation as 'the way we do things around here' (Deal, 1985). It tries to capture the informal, implicit – often unconscious – side of an organisation. Plant's (1987) 'iceberg' model emphasises those aspects of an organisation which are 'below the water' but which, if not taken account of, can undermine the formal and visible ones. Culture consists of patterns of thought, behaviour and artefacts which symbolise and give meaning to the place of work. For the people who work in organisations such as schools and colleges therefore:

Meaning derives from the elements of culture: shared values and beliefs, heroes and heroines (and villains), ritual and ceremony, stories and an informal network of cultural players (Deal, 1985, p. 607).

Rituals, for example, can demonstrate to members what is important about the community to which they belong (Bush, 1998). Schools are rich in rituals such as assemblies and prize-givings but, equally, schools and colleges are likely to have rituals concerned entirely with staff behaviour which are powerful indicators of culture. These might take the form of certain presentations or social events, for example. Human resource managers therefore need to be aware that some behaviour and rituals may have much greater significance for the people involved than is at first apparent.

Activity

At this point, you may find it helpful to note down any special features, in terms of ceremonies or rituals, for example, of your own school or college and consider why these exist and to what extent they typically represent for you the norms of the organisation, in terms of how people are expected to behave.

❑ Effective and ineffective cultures

Handy and Aitken (1986) pointed out that particular cultures were not inherently good or bad, because they are situational. The important point was that cultures should be appropriate to the organisations and the people who work in them. Nevertheless, it is important for the manager to be clear about features of cultures which may contribute to them being more or less effective.

(i) Existence of sub-cultures

Perhaps related to the size of the school or college, the possibility exists of the development of sub-cultures and, inevitably, the possibility of poor communications and relationships or even conflict between them.

In their research into effective departments in secondary schools, Sammons, Thomas and Mortimore (1997) found that the culture of individual departments was one of the key indicators of the differences between more effective and less effective departments, sometimes even in the same school. Significantly, in the more effective schools, 'the school and departmental cultures mirror and reinforce one another' (ibid., p. 172).

(ii) Balance of pressure and support

Schools can be criticised for placing an emphasis on 'caring' *at the expense of* achievement often especially in socially deprived areas. The investigations into a number of schools in poor areas which managed to gain high achievement was recorded in *Success Against the Odds* (NCE, 1993b). Different emphases in school cultures was found to be a key factor in improving achievement, notably a stress on self-esteem, high expectations and a 'you can do it!' approach. Culture may be seen as specifically related to a stated vision or purpose of what the school or college is for. Sammons, Thomas and Mortimore (1997) found that where heads of departments (HODs) thought 'creation of confident, articulate people' was important, 'English results were significantly better than predicted' (p. 173), compared with departments where HODs did not have that aim.

Towards what might be described as the other end of the scale, Hopkins, Ainscow and West (1994) identified 'the promenading school' as one which had a culture of not being interested in change because the school did well and was over-subscribed. A school with a favoured intake may be in danger of a culture of complacency and therefore be ineffective. Stoll and Fink (1998) describe the 'cruising school' as having some of its cultural norms:

Reactive	'Let's wait and see'
Conformity	'Don't rock the boat'
Nostalgia	'Things used to be great round here'

Avoidance of commitment   'Let's send it to a committee!'
Blaming others   'They are pushing new ideas down our throats'

(Stoll and Fink, 1998, p. 194–7)

Each of the two types of schools described above had developed cultures which, for different reasons, placed insufficient emphasis on improving students' achievement. From the manager's point of view, action needed would involve challenge or pressure of some degree. However, Elliott's (1996) research in further education colleges may suggest that too much pressure at senior level may lead to a gap in cultures between those operating directly with the students (i.e. teaching) and those responsible for managing systems in the organisation.

In the chapter on 'Managing staff development' in *Managing People in Education*, Middlewood argues that a culture of extended professionality and planned development opportunities will be most likely to be effective in moving staff forward.

❑ The management of culture

If the culture of a school or college is so important, what are the possibilities for managers in affecting and developing that culture?

Bush (1998) suggests that one tangible way for leaders to generate culture is to focus upon the aims of a school or college since these are meant to be the key ways in which values and beliefs of an organisation are reinforced.

In their study of effective schools and departments, Sammons, Thomas and Mortimore (1997) identified three broad categories of culture at both levels which could usefully act as guidelines for the manager to focus upon in influencing culture in schools and colleges. These are:

(i) **Order** (behaviour – policy and practice). This encompasses a common vision and goals to develop a positive environment, both within and outside the classroom. Patterns of attendance, punctuality, behaviour and motivation will be examples of ways through which this order is effected.

(ii) **Task achievement** (or academic emphasis). The key emphasis again is on a shared agreement that achievement outcomes (such as examination results) are important in assessing effectiveness. High expectations and consistency in approach (e.g. in homework in schools) are typical features of this emphasis.

(iii) **Relationships** (a student-focused approach). This focuses on the students' actual experience of learning and indeed of being at school or college. Students feeling valued as people, feeling cared for, and being satisfied with the experiences are all aspects of this.

Sammons, Thomas and Mortimore (1997) summarise these aspects and their importance by suggesting (p. 174) that 'Task achievement (enabled by an academic emphasis and an orderly environment) needs to be supplemented by an acknowledgement of the importance of individuality, the quality of the learning experience and positive patterns of attendance and behaviour.'

❑ Building on key learning points

- School and college cultures with their emphasis on values, behavioural norms and relationships are important indicators of whether human resource management is contributing to organisational effectiveness.

- Such cultures are likely to have specific features.

- It is possible for managers to identify features upon which they wish to focus.

Section C

6.   Key areas of application

Introduction

This section of the book recognises the fact that, whatever the diversity in culture or attitudes towards commitment, there are certain processes common to all schools and colleges which managers have to address. This is because they are mandatory (manifestly, staff have to be appointed!) or very nearly so (for example, all new staff undergo induction whether it is formally recognised or not). In examining the applications of managing human resources to actual practice, we consider them in chronological stages. This is for convenience only, since as a manager of people performance in school or college, you are likely to be concerned with them all at once. Unless a manager has the luxury of starting from scratch with a brand new school, or department, he/she will 'inherit' staff who will be at different stages already.

This section deals in turn with the management of:

Recruitment:	i.e. managing to get the most appropriate people to apply
Selection:	i.e. managing to obtain the most appropriate person for the job
Induction:	i.e. managing to enable appointees to have the most effective start
Performance review and appraisal:	i.e. managing to gain the best kind of performance from people
Staff development:	i.e. managing to train and develop people for both personal and organisation effectiveness.

Managing recruitment and selection

This section considers:

- the issues influencing strategic recruitment
- the procedures involved in managing recruitment
- the factors involved in rational approaches to managing selection.

At school or college level, a strategic approach to staff recruitment is desirable. The organisation will or should have a vision, through its strategic thinking (see Middlewood, 1998), of how it may be in, say, five or six years time, including its curriculum and what approaches to learning and teaching may be operating. To enable that vision and curriculum to be effectively delivered, what kind of workforce (teaching and associate) will be needed? What minimum level of ICT skills will be needed by staff, for example? Knowing that continuing change is almost certain, is the ability to be flexible and change jobs, learn new as yet unknown skills, a prerequisite for that staff? At another level, Colne Community School in Essex, England, for example, is among those schools which has specified that all associate staff should have a first aider qualification or must obtain it within six months of appointment. This is not only practical but illustrates some forward thinking to a staff where first aid is not something teachers are involved in, leaving them more free to focus on teaching.

As mentioned in the Introduction (p. 2), the distinction between 'associate' and 'teaching' staff is less rigid than once was the case. In an FE college, for example, a workshop supervisor may be engaged in supporting student learning in an open learning centre. This blurring of roles is likely to increase as the emphasis in the twenty-first century moves from teaching to learning.

Hall (1997a, p. 149) suggests that there are some strategic approaches to recruitment which managers need to address:

- how many and what types of people are required
- which of those needs can be satisfied by transfer and development of existing staff
- anticipated problems in recruitment
- the need for a recruitment timetable, so that posts do not remain vacant unnecessarily.

In considering these issues, we suggest five contexts within which recruitment is managed:

❏ 1. Growth and survival

Herriott (1989) identified five trends which were seen as critical in determining whether organisations survive:

- the **quality** imperative
- the **information technology** imperative (especially IT support for decision-making)
- the **evolution** imperative (evolving changes in organisational structures)
- the **communication** imperative (response to external environment)
- the **change** imperative (ability to respond to change quickly).

❏ 2. Succession planning

The second context is the **succession planning** policy of the organisation. Autonomous schools and colleges are becoming more aware of the importance of succession planning. This is the process of managing human resources to enable the organisation's strategic plans to be met. Succession planning involves more than recruitment and selection. It is concerned with anticipating demand and supply and depends on an audit which addresses the organisation's current supply of staff in terms of:

- skills
- experience
- age
- status
- turnover, and, of course,
- cost.

In schools and colleges, where the most important and expensive resource is the staff, the auditing is less easy than in some other types of organisation. For example, good teachers will improve with experience whereas equipment will depreciate with age. Some of the issues involved in the succession planning aspect of recruitment include:

- **Retraining** – is there likely to be a need for existing newly appointed staff to be retrained to meet future demands?

- **Internal promotion** – is there a likelihood of existing or newly appointed staff having to be promoted to more senior posts in the same school or college?

- **Redundancy** – will people recruited now be capable of finding new employment in the light of possible redundancies in the future?

A popular method of forecasting is known as 'scenario planning' where the school or college anticipates its best and worst scenarios by asking questions such as:

- What if a new rival school were to be opened near us in four years time?
- What if our staying-on rate doubled in the next six years?

❑ 3. Labour market

The third context is the **labour market** which requires an awareness of who is available for recruitment. It is tempting for managers to:

(a)   root recruitment and selection procedures in the labour market conditions of yesterday without questioning likely changes in the labour market; and

(b)   assume that macro-employment issues are of marginal relevance to managers in education.

In Britain, for example, although the total working population is forecast to remain relatively stable to the year 2000, there will be a large reduction in the number of young people in the working population, with a consequent decrease in young qualified staff for schools and colleges, and a corresponding increase in older people. This changing emphasis is highlighted by Fidler (1993, pp. 9–10) who gives statistics for the increased number of re-entrants to the teaching profession:

> In 1980–81 re-entrants made up 37 per cent of the inflow. This had risen to 48 per cent by 1983–84 and has remained at around or just over 50 per cent of the inflow since then.

Also, women will account for an increasing proportion of the working population. (See, for example, Marianne Coleman, 'Women in educational management', in *The Principles of Educational Management*.) In addition, given the possible increased competition for graduates from other European countries in the 1990s one can suggest that schools and colleges in Britain will need to ensure their recruitment policies and procedures address this situation.

❑ 4. Legislation

Managing recruitment and selection must be carried out within the framework of the relevant legislation, which includes legislation involving discrimination. In Britain, the Sex Discrimination Act, the Race Relations Act and the Disabled Persons (Employment) Acts all have to be adhered to at the recruitment stage and remain key issues in many areas of managing people. In the USA discrimination on the basis of **age** is forbidden by law at the recruitment stage. Some European countries have similar legislation. Bearing in mind the points made earlier about the presence of more older people and women in the workforce, recruitment managers need to be alert to any assumptions they may have concerning the age profile of candidates for selection they might like to appoint.

Activity

Look at the advertisements for posts in any one issue of one educational publication and ask yourself whether any of them imply assumptions about the gender, race or age of the person sought and, if so, how?

❑ 5. Local conditions

The fifth context is the local or situational one, although 'local' is a relative term, geographically. An important task here is the identification of likely **competitors** for the same candidates, and the effect of that knowledge on recruitment, especially the advertising of vacancies. A second issue is that of **cost**:

● the cost of the post itself; and

● the cost involved in the actual process of recruiting and selecting a person to fill the vacancy.

Undertaking the analytical exercise below should help to clarify your own ideas concerning cost factors in recruitment.

Activity

Choose a 'middle management' post within your own school or college.

- Establish or estimate the annual salary and on-costs for this post.
- Estimate the total cost to the organisation if the person appointed remains on payroll for 5 years.
- Take into account any other cost factors you may be aware of, e.g. settling in expenses, increments, etc.

You then have the cost of the post in terms of what the school or college is investing in over that period.

- Now calculate the cost options involved in advertising (where? in what form?), documentation production and postage,
- travel and subsistence expenses for interviewees and interviewers,
- time of interviewers, etc.

This gives you the cost of making the appointment.

The key cost issue for managers is in weighing the two totals against each other to reach a decision about how much to spend on recruitment.

It will be helpful to repeat the above for appointing a member of the support staff.

❑ Recruitment policies and procedures

A useful starting point is for us to consider an example of an actual recruitment policy taken, in this instance, from a local authority in England.

Recruitment Policy

OUR POLICIES ARE:

1. To recruit the most suitable applicant for the job.

2. To recruit ensuring that no one receives less favourable treatment on the grounds of race, colour, nationality, ethnic or national origins, disability, gender or marital status or is disadvantaged by conditions or requirements which cannot be shown to be justifiable.

3. To treat applicants as valued people keeping them informed of the processes involved and the current state of their application.

4. To use the best methods of assessment available in order to compare applicants' abilities against the job's requirements.

5. To collect and hold only sufficient data to enable the processes to be undertaken and not to use the data for any other unrelated purpose.

6. To undertake all such activities in a professional manner observing the highest possible standards of security, confidentiality and objectivity, whilst operating within the limits of available resources.

(Northamptonshire County Council, 1993)

Such a policy statement has implications for the information provided for potential applicants, arrangements for de-briefing of unsuccessful candidates, the personnel specification for the vacancy concerned and, also, the treatment of internal candidates for the post.

❏ Procedures involved in managing recruitment

1. Defining the vacancy

There are two basic areas to be managed in defining the vacancy:

- describing the job ('job description')
- describing the person who would best fill the job ('person specification').

Several writers on personnel issues suggest an 'exit interview' (i.e. interviewing the person who is leaving to create the vacancy) in order to ascertain why the person is leaving and establish whether the existing job and person specifications are still relevant.

> You must focus on the job to be done, not on the person who used to do it, on the needs of the children and the community, and the balance within the teaching staff as a whole – in the light of your educational aims and the school's development plans. The discussions that take place at this point will set the scene for the whole selection process. Working together as a team with the head, you (the governors) must reach decisions on what exactly you are looking for (Taylor and Hemmingway, 1990, p. 8).

Thomson (1993, p. 12) suggests the following as ways of ascertaining what the job *actually* involves and enabling the job description to be written:

- Question the present job-holder about the job using a written questionnaire.
- Give the present job-holder a list of possible tasks and ask him/her to select those that apply to this job.
- Interview the job-holder.
- Watch the job-holder performing the job.
- Ask other people what they think the job entails.
- Ask the job-holder to keep a diary of everything he/she does in performing the job.
- Do the job yourself for a few days and keep a detailed record.
- Involve the job-holder and his/her supervisor in determining which tasks contribute positively to satisfactory completion of the job and those which inhibit satisfactory job completion (critical incident technique).

2. Person specification

A checklist of competencies associated with effective performance can be devised. We will examine this at the selection stage later.

However, Hackett (1992, p. 35) draws attention to the importance of the behaviour expected of the person when they are actually appointed, rather than personality traits or intellectual capability:

> A more direct approach to establishing just what you need to look for is to consider what the job-holder must be able to *do* – that is, what *abilities* he (sic) needs. If you can match these against the *demands* which the job will make, you are less likely to find that you have recruited someone who is incapable of performing to the required standard. If you also give some thought to the *rewards* which the job offers, in terms of pay and benefits, relationships and job satisfaction, you can then work out what individual *needs* these are likely to satisfy. If you recruit someone whose needs are met by the rewards which the job offers, he (sic) is much more likely to stay and work hard.

This sort of specification provides the **criteria** on which the selection will actually be based.

An interesting and challenging exercise would be to devise a specification for the person required to fill your current post if you were to leave it! Does it have to be someone like you?

3. Other issues

Other issues in recruitment involve:

- the nature of the **contract** (permanent or fixed-term? full-time or part-time? job share?)

- **advertising**
- **information** to be sent to applicants.

Apart from the importance of this information for recruitment purposes, it is important to realise that:

> a request for an application form represents a major opportunity to market the school . . . this opportunity must be firmly grasped (Hume, 1990, p. 40).

In addition, part of the purpose of sending good information is for unsuitable applicants to de-select themselves, for:

> the more information you send to candidates, provided it's relevant and well-presented, then the better able they will be to decide for themselves whether it's the kind of job they're suited for. This can save you – and them – a lot of wasted time (Taylor and Hemmingway, 1990, p. 15).

It is worth emphasising again that in the management of human resources, the recruitment of effective staff is inevitably concerned with certain formal procedures, some of them demanded by legislation and some by organisational 'rules'. Although this is so, the concern for **quality**, **commitment** and **performance** remains central to effective management of these procedures. Procedures offer frameworks within which effective managers perform. Equally, all kinds of key management principles are related which affect the school or college's culture, structure and environment. Hall (1997a, p. 151) stresses the need for managers to be clear whether they are seeking 'human resources' or 'resourceful humans'.

❏ Issues in managing staff selection

The whole process which begins from the moment a potential vacancy is identified is best seen as a continuous one. Selection processes will be managed within the context of an organisation's recruitment policy and induction will be most effective if it is already planned to begin the moment an appointment is confirmed. We suggest there are three issues to be addressed in management of **selection**:

1. Acknowledgement of technical and functional aspects of the roles of staff
By this we mean that the selection has to recognise that it is concerned with:

- **what** an organisation does; and
- **how** it does it.

An organisation will succeed through the knowledge, abilities and skills of those who work in it ('technical' aspects) and the degrees of commitment, motivation and effort with which they apply these attributes ('functional' aspects). The latter are clearly affected by the character and personality of the individual and the culture and structure of the organisation. If both these aspects have to be considered in managing the selection processes, the key question for the organisation's managers is the extent to which both the technical and functional aspects of roles can be determined or assessed.

(a) **Technical aspects**. These are more easily assessed since, for example, the qualifications of candidates will inevitably be based upon knowledge and skills required to obtain them, e.g. through examinations. There are also well-established tests of abilities which can be used (although the key choice for selection managers may lie in determining *which* tests for which abilities will be appropriate). This question of 'selection instruments' will be dealt with later.

(b) **Functional aspects**. The question of assessing the functional aspects of a person, however, is far more complex. It involves judgements about whether the person will 'fit in', their ability to work well in a team or the factors which will motivate them as individuals. Does, for example, the person share the values of the organisation, not merely *say* so? The earlier section on 'Teams' examines much of this issue.

2. The need for objectivity in a potentially very subjective process

Although it is tempting to assume that any subjectivity is bound to be related to functional aspects of the applicant's role (i.e. to their personality), it can easily be found in a failure to be objective about technical aspects. For example, one selector may be in favour of one candidate because he or she has a particular qualification rather than another. Alternatively, too much weight may be given altogether to academic achievement at the expense of other qualities which might be more relevant to effective performance of the job.

The need to bring objectivity to selection management touches upon important areas regarding selection personnel:

- Who should be involved in the process?
- Is training of selectors essential or desirable?
- If training is needed, what skills are required?

Managers will need to assess how helpful is the involvement of lay personnel, such as governors. In self-managing schools and colleges it is common practice for governors, for example, to be involved in staff selection. However, it can be argued that professional managers need training in selection just as much as lay selectors.

If we examine some of the traditional practices which can distort a selection process, it is possible to identify a strong element of subjectivity involved. These practices include:

- basing judgements upon intuition rather than facts
- making 'snap' judgements
- insisting on a personal stereotype of what is a 'good' candidate
- comparing candidates with the previous post-holder or with other candidates rather than the agreed criteria
- preferring a candidate in one's own image.

Selection interviews, for example, have been demonstrated to be unreliable as predictors of performance by psychologists and researchers since the 1920s.

Thomson (1993) summarises the shortcomings as follows:

- Interviewers often make up their minds about a candidate within the first five minutes of the interview and – consciously or unconsciously – spend the rest of the interview trying to justify their judgement.

- Interviewers' judgements of candidates can be affected by their appearance, speech, gender and race either positively or negatively; people tend to favour others whom they perceive to be like themselves.

- Few interviewers have undertaken any training in interview skills.

- Research on memory shows that we remember information we hear at the beginning and end of an interview and, thus, tend to forget vital details and facts given in the middle.

- It is impossible for the human brain to concentrate at the same level over a prolonged period; thus if you are interviewing several candidates on the same day, they may not receive equal amounts of your attention.

- Finally, the British Psychological Society has found that even well-conducted interviews are only 25 per cent better than choosing someone by sticking a pin in a list of candidates!

(Thomson, 1993, p. 30)

It is noteworthy that the above list not only refers to individual prejudices that may occur but also to human factors such as memory and concentration.

Hackett (1992) notes some of the common forms of unconscious intuitive responses as:

(a) **The halo effect**. This occurs where one feature of the interviewee becomes an overriding factor which governs our perception of the person. A common pitfall is to assume that someone who is attractive and articulate is also intelligent.

(b) **Prejudice/bias**. We tend to pre-judge people, either favourably or unfavourably, because they belong to a particular group or remind us of a particular person. Common prejudices include the assumption that members of one race are more hard-working than those of another, or that women are less reliable than men. These preconceptions will colour our interpretation of any comments they make.

(c) **Stereotypes**. These take two forms:

  (i) *Good worker stereotypes*. We may build up a picture in our minds of what a good worker is like, and then use the interview as a means of finding someone who matches that rather than the personnel specification. We will be favourably disposed to those who appear to match, and will be more critical of those who do not match. The most common stereotypes of the good worker are the 'boy scout' stereotype (who is a do-gooder and pillar of the community), and the 'human relations' stereotype (who is a jolly good chap whom everybody likes). Neither may be right for the job.

  (ii) *Physical trait stereotypes*. We may identify one physical characteristic and assume that everyone who possesses that trait will be alike in character. Examples are the assumption that people with red hair have quick tempers and that people whose eyes are close together are not to be trusted. These unfounded assumptions will again colour our judgement and make it more difficult for us to evaluate information in a well-balanced way.

(d) **Unfavourable information**. Most of us are more heavily influenced by people's bad points than by their good ones. Once we have formulated an adverse impression we are slow to change our minds (Hackett, 1992, p. 70).

All these elements of subjectivity indicate the critical need for selection to be managed as objectively as possible. Any process involving humans can never be completely free from some of the above elements, but they can be recognised as such and nullified as much as possible by the process management.

3. Equal opportunities

Legislation will need to be taken account of in:

- advertising
- job description
- person specification.

Similarly, all parts of the selection procedure have to be managed to be sure no candidate is disadvantaged because of race, religion, gender or disability by, for example, requiring application letters to be hand-written which might discriminate against certain disabled candidates. Equally, it is arguable that a test of physical strength for a caretaking post involving portering would discriminate against female candidates. You might like to consider these and other similar questions to help you formulate ways of ensuring equal opportunities are provided throughout the selection process management.

Activity

Devise a method of checking all stages of the recruitment and selection processes to ensure that:

  (i) no candidate will be discriminated against
  (ii) prejudices of selectors will be minimised.

For example, you might devise a checklist of certain criteria against which all procedures are assessed. You may find it helpful to imagine specific scenarios, e.g. an interview candidate who is pregnant, and see if your checklist would hold good.

❏ Managing the process of selection

David Middlewood's chapter on 'Managing recruitment and selection' in *Managing People in Education* gives the background to and details of research undertaken in this field.

We suggest that the key issues to be considering in the management of selection processes are:

- Personnel, i.e. **who** shall be involved in the process?
- Criteria, i.e. **against which standards** shall candidates be assessed?
- Weighting, i.e. the **relative** importance of the different criteria.
- Instruments, i.e. **how** shall the candidates' performance be assessed?
- Matching, i.e. **deciding** on which person is best suited to the post.

1. Personnel

The actual involvement of personnel may be determined through an organisation's selection policy or by the selection procedures normally followed. A head of department or curriculum area may, for example, automatically be involved when the vacancy is in their own area. Equally, deputy heads or vice-principals may be involved for some or all of the process, whilst middle managers may be included in order to gain experience of selection and become proficient in it.

As mentioned earlier, the involvement of lay personnel such as governors may be mandatory but, in any case, the appropriate criteria for participation are the particular perspectives that the personnel involved may bring to the process. The involvement of lay personnel can often bring a valuable, different perspective from that of the professionals working within the organisation.

Finally, the issue of training for those involved in selection needs to be considered.

2. Criteria and weighting

Criteria for selection may include:

- **biographical data** such as qualifications and experience
- **skills** – technical, managerial, etc.
- **knowledge**, e.g. of current legislation, health and safety, curriculum requirements
- **attitudes and values**, e.g. personal ambition, loyalty
- **others** such as interests.

It is in the weighting of the relative importance of the various criteria that the analysis of the job requirements will bear fruit. Bringing together the job description and person specification enables the drawing up of a checklist of selection criteria for all selectors to use **consistently**.

Activity

Devise a criteria checklist – with weightings – for use by selectors in appointing:

(a)   a deputy head or vice-principal of your organisation
(b)   a classroom teaching post
(c)   a secretarial or clerical assistant post.

You will probably find the devising of weightings difficult because of the need to rank elements of the work – it is easy to say that one task is more important than another but rather more difficult to give it a value. However, this is one way in which we can overcome some of the inconsistencies in the selection process.

3. Instruments

'Instruments' are those devices or tools used in structuring the selection process. In that sense, some have already been referred to, such as job descriptions and application forms. We will confine ourselves here to four of the most important:

- interviews
- tests
- exercises
- assessment centres.

(i) Interviews. We suggest that the effective management of interviewing acknowledges the following key principles:

Interviewing is a two-way process. Since candidates can only be appointed on the basis of past performance and potential for future performance, it is important that they have an opportunity to relate their performance to date to the proposed job by, for example, being enabled to concentrate during the interview on describing past life and experience which is relevant to what is needed for the post available (Bolton, 1983).

Consistency in approach by interviewers. This has management implications for choice of personnel involved, training of interviewers, and a clear organisational policy on selection.

Interviewing involves specific skills. Since face-to-face interviewing is obviously a communication process, the skills involved are primarily those of communication.

Riches (1994b), Morgan (1989) and Middlewood (1997b) all refer to the limitations of interview processes.

> A good question is one that encourages the interviewee to answer freely and honestly. A bad question is one that inhibits the interviewee from answering freely or produces distorted information (Southworth, 1990, p. 134).

Interviewing, however, is only part of the selection process. Historically, interviews have been seen as by far the most important part of the process and, in some cases, *all* important. Remembering the inadequacies of interviews, the inevitable risk is that the person appointed may be the person who performs best at interview, not the person who will perform best in the job, although statistically these will sometimes be the same person! In managing selection processes, therefore, we suggest it is important to have an idea of the *relative* importance (or weighting) of the interview, compared with other evidence upon which the assessment for selection will be based, e.g. application letter, reference(s) informal discussion, exercises, etc.

(ii) Tests. Psychometric tests (which can include work sampling, tests of ability or of personality) can be more reliable than interviews as long as two important conditions are fulfilled: firstly, that the test is relevant to the job and, secondly, that the people using the test are trained in its use.

In education, psychometric tests have not been widely used in the past but their use is growing. Technical ability tests are increasingly being used in appointments of technical support staff, for example. In the appointment of senior managers, personality diagnostic tests such as these based on Belbin's work, for example, are used to ascertain the suitability of leaders or potential leaders for working with others.

Our brief extract below comes from a much fuller actual, but for obvious reasons anonymous, report on a candidate for a senior post in the educational world:

Strengths: Strong on critical thinking and objectivity, scoring in the top percentile for verbal reasoning.

Weaknesses: May be hypercritical and seen as intense by others, who may not be inspired by his/her level of drive and management style.

(iii) Exercises. The use of exercises of various kinds is developing in the educational world and examples include:

- **In-tray exercise**: candidates are asked to sift and prioritise and decide action upon a sample of documents.

- **Written report**: having been given certain information, candidates are asked to write a report for a particular audience.

- **Role play simulation**: candidates are asked to enact the job applied for in a particular situation.

- **Oral presentation**: candidates are asked to present formally to the interviewers a brief (usually 5 or 10 minutes) synthesis of their views or approach to a particular issue. Usually, candidates may use visual aids in support of their oral presentation, e.g. slides or overhead projections.

- **Leaderless group discussion**: candidates are grouped together to discuss a topic or reach a decision on a question. Selectors are involved only as observers of individuals' performances with the group's processes. Situations in which the groups are placed are usually co-operative (e.g. the group must come to a consensus on an issue), but operate within a competitive framework.

(iv) Assessment centres.

An assessment centre is a variety of testing techniques designed to allow candidates to demonstrate, *under standardised conditions*, the skills and abilities most essential for success in a given job (Joiner, 1989, p. 182). [our emphasis]

Joiner claims that good assessment centres 'can greatly improve a selection or promotional process particularly for jobs requiring a variety of skills in a variety of situational contexts' (p. 173). Most people would recognise that teaching, for example, fits the job described here!

The centres therefore involve a series of individual and group exercises, observed by trained assessors. All the exercises are set within a common frame of reference (e.g. a set of stated criteria as to suitability for headship), and focus on assessing potential for success at a higher level than the assessee's current job demands.

In summarising the whole issue of instruments available to managers of the selection process, we need to stress again that selection is a person-to-person process and therefore subject to human fallibility. Technical assessment methods are becoming more available and offer scope for greater impartiality, yet the culture and ethos of a particular organisation confirms the necessity for that organisation's representatives to be involved on a personal level via, for example, interviewing.

Morgan (1989) uses the phrase 'black box' to describe the criteria in the process which selectors use but have not explicitly agreed. He concludes that the challenge in managing selection processes is:

how to accommodate requirements which can appear conflicting: the management need for impartial technical assessment methods to gather evidence on candidate fitness for headship; and the need to satisfy the demand for a visible democratic accountability and social legitimation by the local community. The application of the management perspective to selection in other public services has resolved this 'conflict' by ensuring that only those candidates who have satisfied the most rigorous technical assessment and found to be capable of doing the job to a satisfactory minimum level of performance are offered to the 'democratic controllers' for appointment decision (Morgan, 1989, p. 169).

4. Matching

Finally, we come to the stage in the selection process of making a decision about which candidate best matches the requirements of the job. Here the selectors are **assessing** the **performance** of the candidates, through the **instruments** used. At this stage, the selectors will need to assess the **evidence** that has been derived from the instruments.

Southworth (1990) has stressed the importance of applying the following notions to the evidence:

- **adequacy** (how sufficient is it?)
- **integrity** (how truthful and accurate is it?)
- **appropriateness** (how relevant is it?).

Ultimately, as both Middlewood (1997b) and Morgan (1997) point out, the real difficulty lies in establishing a relationship between the selection process as a predictor of effective performance and the actual performance after appointment. Both writers advocate follow-up discussions both informal and formal, because it needs to be recognised that it may be the job that has changed, not necessarily the performer.

❏ **Building on key learning points**

- Schools and colleges should try to adopt a strategic approach to the management of recruitment and selection.

- A rational approach to managing recruitment and selection is more likely to be effective, although the subjective element can never be totally eliminated.

- Fitness for purpose should be the guiding principle in assessing which methods are used for staff selection.

👁 Reading

*Now please read David Middlewood's chapter, 'Managing recruitment and selection' in **Managing People in Education**. This chapter emphasises the need for rational approaches in what is potentially a very subjective area of management judgement.*

Induction

This section considers:

- what induction is and what are its purposes
- what factors affect induction's effectiveness
- the role of the mentor in induction.

Induction is essentially an initiation into the job and the organisation. In the case of newly qualified personnel entering their first posts, it is clearly also an initiation into the profession.

It could be argued that schools and colleges have a moral responsibility to new entrants to the profession: to provide effective induction because of the implications for the education of pupils and students generally, and also because of the costs involved in initial training. In addition, the notion of effective induction and mentoring acquire an additional significance with the move towards school or college-based initial teacher training (ITT) which is discussed in an earlier section.

We believe that any school or college committed to effective management of human resources needs to manage quality induction for all employees taking up new posts. However, it is true to say that more attention has been given to the induction of beginners (NQTs) than other new post-holders (e.g. Earley and Kinder, 1994). The School Management Task Force (DES, 1990) recommended that in England and Wales a programme of induction for senior management be one of the key issues in implementing its recommendations for management development. The focus on senior staff was primarily an acknowledgement that induction for all new post-holders was not possible to achieve quickly and the process should therefore begin 'at the top'.

❑ Purposes of induction

It is possible to identify three major purposes of induction in schools and colleges. These are:

- socialisation
- achieving competence
- exposure to institutional culture.

1. Socialisation

The so called 'socialisation' of inductees is perhaps the most important issue in induction in effective organisations. Schein (1978) identified five elements in this process:

(i) Accepting the reality of the organisation (i.e. the constraints governing individual behaviour).

(ii) Dealing with resistance to change (i.e. the problems involved in getting personal views and ideas accepted by others).

(iii) Learning how to work realistically in the new job, in terms of coping with too much or too little organisation and too much or too little job definition (i.e. the amount of autonomy and feedback available).

(iv) Dealing with the boss and understanding the reward system (i.e. the amount of independence given and what the organisation defines as high performance).

(v) Locating one's place in the organisation and developing an identity (i.e. understanding how an individual fits into the organisation (Schein, 1978, pp. 36–7).

Two implications for managers arise from this. The first is that the influence, reactions and attitudes of peers, managers and other employees have a significant impact on the success or otherwise of the induction. Secondly, the performance of the new person, and thereby the performance of the organisation, will be affected by the success of that induction.

2. Achieving competence

In learning how to perform in the new post, Kakabadse, Ludlow and Vinnicombe (1987) suggest that the inductee's cycle will have three stages:

(i) **Getting used to the place**, i.e. overcoming the initial shock and immobilisation of the new organisation and job demands.

(ii) **Re-learning**, i.e. recognising that new skills have to be learned or how learned skills have to be re-applied.

(iii) **Becoming effective**, i.e. consolidating one's position in the organisation by applying new behaviours and skills or integrating newly formed attitudes with ones held from the past (Kakabadse, Ludlow and Vinnicombe, 1987, p. 8).

3. Exposure to institutional culture

Hunt (1986) argues that the most important facet of induction is the 'transfer of loyalties to the new organisation' (p. 213). The issue of loyalties is associated with the school or college's culture and values and, as such, it will have been addressed in the management of the recruitment and selection process. For the successful candidate, the induction process begins immediately after accepting the post.

This aspect of induction is probably much less common, however, for support staff in schools and colleges. As Paisey (1985) remarks: 'Regrettably, for non-teaching staff this approach is rarely pursued. There is a dearth of provision' (p. 175). Mortimore *et al.* (1994) also found provision very spasmodic.

Similarly, induction is rarely provided for temporary or part-time staff: 'in the misguided belief that they will not care much about the organisation and that they are just there to do the job' (Thomson, 1993, p. 110).

Activity

You may find it useful at this stage to note down:

(1) how you felt and how you were helped at the start of your first post;
(2) how you felt and how you were helped at the start of your present post;
(3) how your school or college inducts newly qualified staff.

You might be helped by using the Kakabadse *et al.* typology as a framework. To see how others feel about the same organisation, interview two recently appointed full-time and part-time colleagues about their experience of induction.

In all probability you will find that the larger the organisation the more varied the experience – a reflection of the way in which interpersonal relationships build up. There are, however, ways of overcoming this hit-and-miss approach. It is to these we now turn.

❏ Managing effective induction

Induction may involve some or all of the following:

- preparatory visits to the school or college prior to starting
- obtaining information about the school or college
- identifying the needs of the inductee in order to plan to meet them
- offering guidance and support over personal (e.g. family) issues related to taking up the new appointment
- allocating a specific person (mentor) to support the person during induction
- (in larger institutions) arranging off-site programmes for all new employees together.

Schools and colleges need to make decisions about the management of induction which reflect their own values and priorities as organisations:

Socialisation and cultural integration. The degree to which this should be part of any formal programmes is debatable and is a sensitive area. Issues such as appropriate forms of dress, how people are addressed, and informal communications networks within the institution are less contentious and will also arise during the early period in the post.

How long should the induction last? Employment legislation in many countries means that all appointments are made on a probationary or trial basis, pending satisfactory performance. Schools and colleges need to decide whether the induction period should coincide with this or, alternatively, end naturally when the need for support is deemed to be no longer there.

Assessment. Linked with the above point is the issue of whether induction should involve assessment of performance or whether policy should specify that the two be kept separate.

Internal promotions. People who change posts within the same school or college may be considered to have a need for and entitlement to some form of induction. This form of induction may well differ from that provided for those new to the organisation.

There are also particular issues with regard to teaching which affect the management of induction:

- Teaching is essentially an autonomous job. However strong the support, the new person is 'on their own' and classes cannot be set aside while the inductee learns.
- There is insufficient time to offer support, especially 'on the job' support.
- Mistakes made in teaching cannot be taken back and wiped out.

We suggested earlier that ensuring effective performance was a central issue for those managing induction. Kakabadse (1983) argues that performance is directly related to attitudes to learning, both of the new person and of those around them. Indeed, outside education, numerous studies have shown that the induction method affects both the rate of turn-over in the first six months and the rate of integration (Hunt, 1986, p. 213).

❏ Mentoring

One of the commonest ways in which schools and colleges attempt to make induction effective is by using mentors. In her chapter 'Managing induction and mentoring' in *Managing People in Education*, Marianne Coleman explores this in detail.

If induction works well, the performance of the newly appointed member of staff will be effective as soon as possible (no precise time period can be specified, of course). The need for the staff member to be managed so that effective performance is maintained and developed is now the issue for the manager. Table 6.1 sets out the different issues involved in the process of mentoring and that of the line manager responsible for performance.

The argument for mentoring in terms of effective human resource management depends upon the following assumptions:

- The best context for growth is where a person is valued as an individual and as a colleague.
- Individuals do not develop in isolation – feedback is essential.
- Each step in development begins with a review of where a person is now.
- It is not a sign of weakness to ask for help. Rather, a request for help is an indication of a healthy climate of trust and commitment to personal growth.
- 'Mutual learning' relationships in an educational organisation are of benefit to individuals and to the schools and colleges in which they work.

Table 6.1 Distinction between mentor and line manager

	Mentoring	**Line Management**
Who	Colleague/peer	Line manager/superior
Nature	Formative	Summative
Purpose	Facilitate development of new skills	Judge performance
Accountability and reporting	To mentee	To own superior
Decisions arising	Responsibility of mentee	Head of institution
Climate	Trusting to experiment and practice, including risk of failure	Tendency to accord with required practices
Data accumulated	Belong to mentee	Filed in personnel records
Agenda topics	Determined by mentee	May be negotiated but agreed within context of organisation's requirements
Value judgement	Drawn out from mentee	Made by line manager
Role of partner	Negotiated with mentee	Determined according to line manager's role
Involvement	Togetherness/partnership	Supervisor/subordinate relationship
Communication	Two-way, questioning	Report, commenting etc.

(Adapted from Middlewood, 1994)

However, while mentoring is often linked with the process of induction, it is important to note that mentoring as a support and developmental process can have value throughout an organisation. 'All teaching and non-teaching staff would benefit from an effective system of mentoring which provides work-related guidance and support' (Smith, 1993, p. 2). As Coleman (1997, p. 161) notes, mentoring is used in so many different contexts that there is no universal agreement on how the role is developed. Research on mentoring of middle managers (Bush *et al.*, 1996) included its use to encourage interdependent working. It could legitimately be seen to offer potential in HRM terms to move towards an involvement strategy, as discussed earlier.

It is likely that using whole institutional mentoring in this way should be seen as an evolutionary process. Ehrich (1994), in pointing out some of the difficulties of institutionalised mentoring, highlights unwilling participation as a potential problem and recommends a programme which is not imposed and not threatening. Megginson and Clutterbuck (1997, p. 236) suggest that mentoring best grows 'organically – out of natural processes of affiliation and support that develop between people, and out of small pilot schemes.'

Activity

Consider the following questions:

How are mentors chosen in your own institution? What skills do they appear to need and do some do the job more effectively than others? Does mentoring exist apart from the induction process?

❏ Building on key learning points

- Induction involves both professional competency and social adjustment.
- Structured induction is more likely to be effective.
- Mentoring is different from line management.

◉ Reading

Please read Marianne Coleman's chapter 'Managing induction and mentoring' in **Managing People in Education.** *This chapter concentrates mainly on the induction of newly qualified teachers but also examines evaluations of induction schemes.*

Performance review and appraisal

This section considers:

- the place of appraisal in any overall management of performance
- the usual components of appraisal schemes
- the tensions inherent in such schemes
- issues affecting its effective application in education.

The educational world was slow in coming to incorporate formal appraisal systems into its management operations, compared with the business world. Appraisal schemes for school teachers and for lecturers in further and higher education in England and Wales were not introduced until the 1990s. The effectiveness of such schemes was limited, largely because, owing to their being statutory and therefore imposed, they were introduced essentially as 'bolted-on' features of management. Evaluations of the teacher scheme (Barber, Evans and Johnson, 1995; Middlewood *et al.*, 1995; Wragg *et al.*, 1996) showed that only in a small number of schools was appraisal properly linked with school development planning and staff development programmes. The failure to share individual targets at school level highlighted the tension between the individuals' fear of loss of confidentiality and the obvious need for the organisation to know how individual aims fitted with its overall direction.

Any appraisal scheme, therefore, is best seen as part of the management of performance of individuals in the school or college. The need for such review of performance is clear and based on a few common-sense assumptions about people management, i.e. that most people perform best when:

- they know what is required of them
- they receive guidance and support when necessary
- they receive feedback about their performance
- they are clear about the outcomes of the feedback.

 Reading

Please read the chapter 'Managing appraisal' in* Managing People in Education *by David Middlewood which examines the components of appraisal schemes in detail. Both this chapter and 'Managing individual performance' by Keith Foreman conclude that it is the management of staff as people/persons that is crucial if performance management for the organisation is to be effective, whether by ensuring appraisal is fully integrated into other aspects of managing the organisation's people (Middlewood, 1997a, p. 183) or by reconciling the concerns for teacher as professional and as person (Foreman, 1997, p. 218).

Management of performance then can be described as consisting of these broad stages:

1. **Planning**. The overall objective at this stage is to enable staff to be clear about what is expected of them and why, e.g. a performance contract.

2. **Managing**. At this stage, the manager's objective is to encourage the staff member to deliver what has been agreed, through both monitoring and supportive strategies, e.g. 'developmental mentoring' (Cardno and Piggot-Irvine, 1997).

3. **Appraising/reviewing**. Here, the manager takes stock of what has been achieved but with an emphasis on future performance.

4. **Follow-up**. This stage may involve specific 'rewards' but specific action plans are essential to ensure the process is continuous.

❏ Reviewing/appraising performance

In developing effective management of the actual process of appraising performance, managers should be conscious of tensions inherent in the process which they need to reconcile.

The **first** may be described as 'evaluation for accountability versus personal development'.

Staff in schools or colleges must be accountable for their performance as professionals – to line managers, to school or college governors, to regional authorities, to taxpayers, but, above all, to their students. This accountability has to be assessed in some way through actual 'results' of their actions. At the same time, they have an entitlement to personal professional development which is a vehicle through which they will continue to improve their performance. Cardno and Piggot-Irvine (1997) argue that only an approach which integrates the two will be effective, and suggest elements in schemes which tend to focus on one or the other (see Figure 6.1).

Accountability	Development
Performance contracts	Professional development
Job descriptions	Plans
Targets	Developmental mentoring
Appraisal interviews	Self-evaluation
Student evaluation	Peer evaluation

Figure 6.1 The tension between accountability and development (adapted from Cardno and Piggot-Irvine, 1997)

We should note, of course, that some accountability issues, involving those of basic competence and misconduct, are managed separately (see Keith Foreman's chapter in *Managing People in Education* for a discussion of these).

The **second** tension relates closely to this and concerns the kind of data which are relevant and fair to gather for a review of performance, i.e. quantitative versus qualitative.

Quantitative data, such as examination results and retention rates, are easy to gather and superficially easy to analyse. The relationship between such data and rewards, for example, can be straightforward. However, the process of teaching and learning involves many factors which do not lend themselves to this and relationships with students, for example, which are essential to effective learning need to be considered.

The **third** tension is what David Middlewood in his chapter on 'Managing appraisal' in *Managing People in Education* calls 'transactional versus transformational'. In other words, the overall process of education (transformation), especially in statutory schooling, is greater than the sum of all the individual lessons (transaction) and some acknowledgement of this needs to be there in the review of overall performance. The key to this probably lies in the context within which appraisal takes place. Hodgson (1996) found that appraisal was more likely to support school improvement where 'it is seen as individual review in the context of school/department/key stage review' (p. 33).

Activity

At this point, you would find it helpful to analyse the appraisal situation in your own school or college, asking yourself:

- Is our system mainly evaluation or developmental or integrated?
- Which elements relate to accountability? Which to development?
- What data are collected and what is the balance between quantitative and qualitative?
- How is individual appraisal linked with organisational or sectional review?

Does the total picture received from appraisals miss out some of the overall educational (transformational) elements expressed, for example, in the organisation's aims?

❑ Different forms of appraisal

The most common form is where appraisal is carried out by the person who has responsibility for the overall performance of the individual, i.e. a line manager. Another form is that of peer appraisal, and a third is known as '360 degree' evaluation. 'In this situation not only feedback from staff (including non-teaching staff) who work for you is sought but also those who are your colleagues as managers, and your superiors. Such an approach gives a full picture of an individual's performance' (Cardno and Piggot-Irvine, 1997, p. 106).

It is worth stressing that, whoever are the appraisers, the *method* of choosing them is critical to the success of the eventual pairing. Whichever method is used, it should be open, publicly documented and consistently applied.

❑ Components of appraisal systems

While schemes vary considerably, whether they be evaluative or developmental, or a mixture of both, there is almost universal agreement that any appraisal will need to include the following:

(a) **Some form of self-review** through which the appraisee makes judgements about his or her own performance. This can be verbal but can make use of an organisation's standardised pro-forma. This pro-forma may be merely a set of prompt questions or a detailed checklist. It may also include the appraisee's own ideas for improving future performance.

(b) **Some collection of data about the appraisee**. These can include both **quantitative** (e.g. attendance and punctuality records) and **qualitative** (e.g views of other people affected by the appraisee's performance) data. Sensitive management issues here concern appropriate sources of information, the type and detail of information sought, and the need to avoid 'gossip'.

(c) **Observation of the appraisee at work**. It would seem foolish to envisage appraising someone's performance without actually **seeing** them at work, but there are difficulties. The essentially passive nature of some activities (e.g. working at a keyboard!) and the private nature of others (e.g. teaching) clearly affect the validity of conclusions drawn from any observation of them.

(d) **Interview meeting between appraiser and appraisee**. This interview serves quite a different purpose from the selection interview we examined earlier. Here, three different types of interview can be identified (after Maier, 1976):

- In the **'tell and sell'** method, the manager directs the interview and gains the acceptance of the appraisee to take steps to improve performance.
- The **'tell and listen'** style requires the manager to give authentic feedback but then to allow the appraisee to respond. Communication and understanding may be much improved. Changes in performance, however, depend upon a change of attitude following improved communication.
- The **'problem-solving'** style as the name implies requires both appraiser and appraisee jointly to acknowledge problems and to work on them together (Fidler, 1988, p. 10).

(e) **Targets being set**. In the introduction to this unit, we identified **targets** under both 'Commitment' and 'Performance' as being one of the crucial elements in the effective management of human resources in educational organisations. Targets being set as part of an appraisal scheme are valuable because they are recognised by the organisation and carry an explicit commitment to action related to them.

(f) **Follow up**. Unless action is taken to follow up issues identified through the appraisal, there can be no improvement in performance. Clearly, this has resource implications, in both financial and human terms. As far as appraisal of teachers is concerned, advice was given in various local education authorities in England and Wales, that a sum of money should be earmarked to meet outcomes of the appraisal process.

❑ Special issues for appraisal in education

Six significant issues arise for the management of appraisal in educational organisations. We need to examine these carefully in considering how to appraise performance most effectively in schools and colleges.

1. Teaching is a very autonomous and individual task. No two teachers are the same; teaching is an occupation in which performance is affected very much by the individual nature and personality of the person concerned.

2. Teaching is a multi-task job. There are, therefore, particular difficulties in assessing the effectiveness of carrying it out.

3. Education involves uncertainty over measurement of results. Outcomes are unclear and, furthermore, are dependent not upon the staff directly but upon the achievements of those for whom the organisation exists, i.e. the students, however those achievements are measured.

4. In education there are no clearly defined 'rewards' in the business sense.

5. There are no simple means of attributing the 'results' obtained by students to specific teacher performance. The concept of value-added measures of performance (see **People or Performance**) remains controversial in education.

6. There are a considerable number of stakeholders in education and, even where a teacher has a line manager, there are a number of other people who have a direct interest in the teacher's performance.

Prior to teacher appraisal being introduced in England and Wales, research projects and pilot studies strongly emphasised the need for positive approaches. In a summary of these studies, Montgomery and Hadfield (1989) found that:

- an emphasis on being positive and constructive in comments on teaching performance was critical to the success of appraisal
- because a teacher's personality and self-image were so evident in classroom performance, any comments were inevitably construed as very personal in nature
- a concentration on weaknesses rather than identified strengths simply led to hostility and negative reaction.

❏ Conditions for effective performance review and appraisal

Poster and Poster (1993) suggest that no single system of appraisal can ever achieve all the potential benefits. 'The climate and circumstance of the organisation will determine which of the potential benefits might realistically be achieved and which could not be accommodated' (p. 153). Hodgson (1996) suggests that the *explicit* support of the head/principal, the resourcing and a realistic action plan are critical.

The climate in which it takes place is vitally important. If data, for example, are to be collected from a variety of sources it is critical that staff understand *why*, e.g. (Jones and Mathias, 1995, p. 33):

- Teaching is a complex activity and performance needs to be appraised from a number of perspectives.
- Performance on a single occasion may not be representative of overall performance.
- The process of triangulation allows for a cross-check of performance.
- The process of data collection should reflect the balance of the job description.

We would add, implied by much written above, that the training of appraisers in the relevant skills is essential. The development gained through such training – in observation, interviewing, for example – is of course of benefit to the appraiser as well as appraisee, and therefore the school or college as a whole gains anyway.

❏ Managing unsatisfactory performance

Situations will inevitably arise where, after support and remedial measures have been tried, a management decision has to be reached that the employee's poor performance is damaging the organisation and the contract needs to be terminated. Similarly, where relations between employer and employee deteriorate, the employee may feel threatened or victimised and be in 'grievance' against the organisation. The whole area therefore of grievance and discipline is one which a manager needs to be aware of and be ready to address. If the principal, senior management and lay personnel involved, such as governors, fail to manage unsatisfactory performance adequately, the overall quality and effectiveness of staff management will be impaired. Therefore, an organised approach is necessary and should incorporate elements such as:

- An appreciation of the need for well-constructed, regularly revised grievance and disciplinary procedures introduced after consultation with staff members and trade unions and professional associations.

- Correct operation of these procedures, including full understanding and agreement on the roles each party (e.g. school management and governing bodies) will play in these procedures.
- An understanding of the rules of natural justice and how they apply in these situations.
- An awareness that grievance and disciplinary procedures are essentially problem-solving tools.
- An approach to dealing with dismissal cases based on reasonable belief, reasonable grounds and reasonable investigation.

(Adapted from Hume, 1990, pp. 48–9.)

Grievance and discipline issues do not take place in isolation and failure to manage them effectively may have far-reaching effects on staff morale, commitment and motivation. For example, the context of the labour market may mean that there is pressure on managers to make the best of current members of staff and, where there are inadequacies, to take positive steps to help the individuals overcome them.

Drucker (1988, p. 140) argues that service institutions, such as schools and colleges, should not employ their ablest people to defend that which has no purpose, e.g. poor performance. Service institutions cannot afford to be paid for 'promises or, at best, for efforts' (ibid.). A high concern for performance is as relevant to the health of service institutions as other organisations. It is essential that dealing with unsatisfactory performance within the school or college is perceived as a positive management action and not the negative one that it is automatically deemed to be. Drucker implies that the true test of an organisation is the way in which it manages, and is seen to manage, unsatisfactory performance.

👁 Reading and Activity

Please read pages 203–12 of Keith Foreman's chapter 'Managing individual performance' in **Managing People in Education.**

List the approaches taken towards managing unsatisfactory performance in your own institution. We suggest you divide them into formal and informal. How much consistency do you find in the informal processes?

❑ Building on key learning points

- Appraisal by its nature can create a tension between evaluation and development.
- Appraisal in schools and colleges is most effective if it is concerned with growth and development.
- Performance is reviewed informally as well as in formal processes.
- Performance needs to be managed so that there is evidence of achievement.
- Managers need to analyse under-performance carefully to understand reasons for it.
- Unsatisfactory performance needs to be managed in a way that sees its outcomes as positive.

Staff development

This section considers:

- the context within which staff development thrives
- the management issues in formal staff development programmes
- more informal ways in which staff development occurs.

If schools and colleges are to become effective learning organisations (see earlier section on 'The Learning Organisation'), then the management of the organisation to enable staff to learn effectively is central. Morally, since learning is the core purpose of schools and colleges, the imperative might be said to be even greater than in some other types of organisations. The link with the preceding section on reviewing and appraising performance is also clear. If such a review is to lead to continuous improvement, from whatever base, then the provision of effective professional development for staff is both an entitlement for the individual and a prerequisite for the organisation. Since a number of terms are used in connection with training or development in teaching, it will be useful to summarise them:

- **Teacher competency** refers to any single knowledge, skill or professional value position, which is relevant to successful teaching practice.

- **Teacher competence** refers to the repertoire of competences a teacher possesses. Overall competence is a matter of the degree to which a teacher has mastered a set of individual competencies.

- **Teacher performance** refers to what a teacher does on the job rather than to what he or she can do. Teacher performance is specific to the job situation.

- **Teacher effectiveness** refers to the effect that a teacher's performance has on students.

- **Effectiveness** depends not only on competence and performance but also on the response students make.

❑ Culture and values of staff development

The development of individual staff, whilst important, needs to be seen by the manager of staff development in the context of whole school/college development. Increasingly autonomy for schools and colleges, whilst offering opportunities for growth and independence, also holds the threat of fragmentation between organisations which proves so damaging within them. Aspinwall and Pedler (1997, p. 240), noting this, state that 'Schools that develop the learning potential of individuals and of teams, have an understanding of the whole school as an organisation and are also aware of their place in, and responsibilities to, the wider community will have much to contribute.'

 Reading

Please read David Middlewood's chapter, 'Managing staff development', in **Managing People in Education.** *He argues that the culture created in a school or college is the vital factor in professional development. This culture will provide opportunities for development, some very structured, some informal. The manager's task may be to ensure that structured opportunities for development are in place and relevant through policies and programmes, and also to support and encourage the informal ones. As with any management process, there needs to be a set of values which underpin the school's or college's approach to the development of the staff who work in it. This approach will guide the stated rationale for the organisation's policy, the planned implementation and evaluation of its formal programmes and also indicate something of the way in which it is believed informal learning can occur. Perhaps these values can be ascertained by asking questions as in the following activity.*

Activity

Consider your answers to these questions:

- Does our organisation support the development of individual staff as *persons*?

- Is there an inclusive organisational approach which includes associate staff as well as teaching staff?

- Is equal emphasis placed on those who are enthusiastic for development and those most needing help or persuasion?

- Is critical self-reflection encouraged?

- Is there a balance between individual career development and organisational improvement?

- Is the underlying message on supporting development and/or remedying deficiency?

- Whatever the answers to these questions and other similar ones, they will give an indication of the coherence – or lack of it – of values underpinning the school's or college's staff development.

❑ Management of provision

The two aspects here will be *what* is provided and *how* it is provided. Middlewood (1997c) argues that recognition of adult learning attitudes and styles is essential for managers, because, for adults 'unlearning' is difficult and present practice is embedded in experience which many staff will have seen as effective until now. This argument, of course, supports the notion of an appropriate culture for development but may also have to be acknowledged in aspects of the provision of the formal programme.

(a) Formal programmes

This process for managers may be seen to consist of:

- identifying needs and prioritising
- planning programmes and activities
- implementation and monitoring
- evaluating the programmes.

(i) Identifying needs and prioritising. *Whose* needs? Needs for development may exist at institutional and individual levels and also within 'sub-units' (Bush, 1995a, p. 4) involving faculties, departments, teams and groups in the external environments. Additionally, there may be a need for the training and development of school or college governors (Esp, 1991).

The issue of *where* these needs are best located, and subsequently prioritised, is not straightforward. Some teachers will have various roles in their schools and colleges. Which should take priority? The potential for role conflict is therefore considerable (Hall, 1997b). In the case of associate staff who are located in specialist areas, such as Learning Support, there may be some occasions when their need is for technical development and others where their needs as members of a group of staff who are 'non-teaching' are paramount.

These issues raise questions of values which may underpin the overall strategy for managing human resources. Additionally, imperatives arising from government requirements may be seen as having to override those needs which the individual school or college feels are crucial.

	Know/can do	Don't know/can't do
Know		
Don't know		

Figure 6.2   Identifying development needs (adapted from Oldroyd and Hall, 1991, p. 67)

How are needs identified? At all levels, needs are most likely to be acted upon if they are recognised by the individuals or groups concerned. Diagnostic documents, adaptations of the organisational or departmental audit, questionnaires and personal interviews are all methods used successfully. Oldroyd and Hall (1991) offer an adaptation of the Johari window to help people recognise their needs (see Figure 6.2).

Activity

Try to complete the boxes in Figure 6.2 in this way:

(i) List in the top left box some aspects of your knowledge and competence that you are confident you have (i.e. what you know and can do).

(ii) List in the top right box those areas of knowledge and competence that you know you do not have (i.e. what you know you don't know/can't do).

This is a useful starting point. If possible, share with a colleague or mentor his/her perceptions of what might go in the other boxes (i.e. bottom left: what I don't know/can do, bottom right: what I don't know that I don't know/can't do).

It is, of course, the bottom right that is the most challenging!

Prioritising. Given the range of needs mentioned above and pressures from various directions, it is essential that the staff development programme is part of the school's or college's overall strategic plan (long-term) and development/business plan (short/medium-term.) This assists the manager in prioritising. Ryan's model, described in David Middlewood's chapter on 'Managing staff development', is a simple example of a school prioritising school, professional and individual development and any such model can be helpful in demonstrating to staff the school's or college's priorities. The explicitness of such models is important, reinforcing the point that improving learning and teaching is the ultimate purpose of all development.

(ii) Planning programmes and activities. Research by Joyce and Showers (1980) and Kinder, Harland and Wootten (1991) suggest a link between the method and content of activities provided with regard to their effectiveness. The recognition of different learning styles for adults may thus be critical in planning the overall programme, which therefore may include a full range of activities, including:

- staff-led workshops
- paired observations
- seminars
- projects
- visits
- courses (external and institution-based).

(iii) Implementing and monitoring. Monitoring the implementation is basically asking the question: 'Are we carrying out what we planned to do?' but may carry elements of formative evaluation: 'Do we need to adjust our plans?' Areas to be monitored include satisfaction with the activity, suitability of the provider, cost-effectiveness, and appropriateness of the actual facilities.

(iv) Evaluating the programmes. The aspects above are relatively easy to evaluate, even at the summative stage, but, since the *ultimate* purpose relates to improvement in practice related to learning and teaching, consideration needs to be given to this. This has proved elusive for many schools and colleges because (a) effective learning is covert not overt and (b) such improvements may take a long time to show their true effect.

You may wish to reflect upon what methods are used in your organisation to monitor and to evaluate the process of the staff development programme and, more challengingly, whether those areas are ones where a longitudinal method of assessing the impact of certain training or development activities upon student learning could be devised!

(b) More informal programmes
Outside of formal programmes, planned and managed, lie many other opportunities for staff development. Collaborative cultures, widely accepted as the most effective for student learning, involve strong professional relationships between staff, teachers talking to each other about students regularly, self-reflection and other daily activities which help to build the critical communities within which professional learning may be 'a natural process which is often unplanned, unremarked and undocumented' (Day, 1995, p. 110).

However, there are a number of ways in which managers can encourage development for staff in semi-structured ways which are essentially 'in-house', and which, with support, lead individuals to contribute towards that critical community.

❑ Mentoring and critical friendships

Mentoring was discussed earlier in the section on induction and can play a crucial role. Above all, mentoring should not be seen as 'soft'. Megginson and Clutterbuck (1997, p. 13) define mentoring as ' "off-line" (by which is meant "not line management") help by one person to another in making significant transitions in knowledge, work or thinking.' They suggest that skilled mentors can make the distinction between getting immediate results and taking a wider view. 'The message becomes clear as the meeting progresses' (ibid., p. 14). One of their powerful arguments is that a mentor can provide stability in an unstable situation. For example, where one person changes jobs within an institution, the mentor does not change because he or she is linked with induction into the new post but remains the stable point of support for the person who may now have a new line manager (ibid., p. 237).

If a mentor is, according to Thomson (1993, p. 111), someone, usually a work colleague at the same or a higher level than the individual, for whom he or she is responsible, to whom the individual can go to discuss work-related issues, there is a sense in which the mentoring relationship is similar to that of the 'master–pupil' relationship in medieval times; the pupil is learning from the mentor's experience and the mentor's role is to encourage and nurture his or her protégé. Mentors can pass on practical insight derived from experience and can pick up on new ideas and attitudes. They can help their protégés to set themselves realistic expectations and steer them in the right direction as far as their career aspirations are concerned. It can, and should, be a mutually rewarding experience.

Many people value being able to pass on what they know, particularly when this is appreciated and others benefit from their knowledge and experience. Clearly the whole organisation can benefit from a system of mentoring. Managers, however, would have reservations about institutionalised mentoring because of unwilling participants, and the relationship between the individuals concerned is critical. The earlier table (6.1, p. 75) on the differences between mentor and line manager suggests that some different skills will be needed by mentors in their different contexts.

In any case, apart from the support for development of individual staff, critical friendships, defined by Day (1995, p. 123) as 'practical partnerships entered voluntarily, based upon a relationship between equals', can bring to the whole organisation advantages such as those listed earlier.

However, many of these informal processes demand time and Healy and Calveley (1998, p. 30) are clear that 'mentoring will not achieve its objectives unless there are clear time allowance for such activities; since time equates to resources, it is questionable whether such resources will be made available.'

As mentioned in the section on reviewing performance, such support can be more specific, such as Cardno and Piggot-Irvine's 'developmental mentoring'. Here the aim is for the mentor to work with the appraisee to help him/her achieve specific targets. Here the activity is likely to include:

- observation of teaching or other performance
- analysis of data collected

85

- discussion of the findings
- setting goals

(based on Cardno and Piggot-Irvine, 1997).

However, the essential link between all these strategies is that they are voluntarily entered into. The manager's task is to encourage as appropriate and, when they are entered into, ensure the professional relationship and agreement has structure and relevance. There may be verbal or even written agreements in some cases.

❏ Practitioner research

Often as part of accredited programmes offered by higher education institutions, a number of staff may carry out 'in-house' research into some aspects of their or their team's work. This research may be classroom focused, and Hopkins, Ainscow and West (1994), for example, argue that this is the key to school improvement. Alternatively, it may be an investigation into any aspect of management or leadership, curriculum, external relations or resourcing of the school or college. The impact on the individual can be twofold. Firstly, the staff member learns something of his/her or team practice which can form the basis for an improvement and, equally important, the individual 'learns how to learn', reflecting on current practice and applying the process to other aspects of work.

Additionally, if such research becomes widespread in an organisation, the impact upon its culture can be considerable. Middlewood and Parker (1998) describe such an impact on an 11–18 secondary school, drawing attention to the spread of enthusiasm and self-motivation among staff, the collaborative spirit engendered and the huge increase in confidence of staff 'as learners'.

❏ Building on key learning points

- Staff development provision and opportunities will be significantly influenced by the general culture and values of the school or college.

- How provision is made is as important as the provision itself.

- Formal programmes should be carefully structured.

- Informal processes play an equally important role.

- Your own piece of research will play an important part in your development and probably in your organisation's!

---

7. Conclusion

The final paragraphs of the preceding section will, we hope, provide for many of you the encouragement to apply what you have read in this book to the management of people in schools and colleges. We would stress that the most important people in these schools and colleges are, of course, the children, pupils and students themselves! Schools and colleges exist for them and their learning and the task of all adults who work in these places is to facilitate and enhance that learning. This applies equally to those who provide the food, keep the place clean and maintain the buildings and to those who lead, manage, teach and tutor. We have deliberately not put in a separate section on the management of staff 'other than teachers', and we believe you will find that most of the sections have relevance to *all* members of staff whatever their role. Certainly, our premise at the beginning of the book concerning **quality, commitment** and **performance** has no exceptions.

The effectiveness of human resource management in its broadest terms obviously needs to be monitored and evaluated but is beyond the scope of this book, although we have addressed the monitoring and evaluation of specific aspects throughout. In terms of your school or college context, monitoring and evaluation will take place against the priorities and objectives which have been set within your institution. We suggest, however, that HRM processes in schools and colleges are only successful to the extent that:

- **monitoring** demonstrates a consistency of approach between strategy, policy and implementation; and
- **evaluation** demonstrates quantifiable improvements in the quality of teaching and learning.

The process of HRM is, quite rightly, open to interpretation, assimilation and development according to the needs of the individual institution. In the final analysis, however, the outcomes have to be measured in terms of how HRM practice has contributed to the quality of learning.

References

Acker, S. (1994) *Gendered Education*, Buckingham: Open University Press.

Argyris, C. (1991) Teaching smart people how to learn, *Harvard Business Review*, May–June, pp. 99–109.

Argyris, C. and Schon, D. A. (1978) *Organizational Learning*, Reading, Massachusetts: Addison Wesley.

Armstrong, M. (1994) *A Handbook of Personnel Management Practice 2/e*, London: Kogan Page.

Aspinwall, K. and Pedler, M. (1997) Schools as learning organisations, in Fidler, Russell and Simkins, *op. cit.*

Atkinson, P. (1990) *Creating Culture Change*, London: IFS Publications.

AUT (1995) *Woman*, no. 36, Autumn, p. 3.

Bangar, S. and McDermott, J. (1989) Black women speak, in H. De Lyon and F. Widdowson Migniuolo (eds.) *Women Teachers: Issues and Experiences*, Milton Keynes: Open University Press.

Barber, M., Evans, A. and Johnson, M. (1995) *An Evaluation of the National Scheme of School Teacher Appraisal*, London: DFEE.

Beard, D. (1993) Learning to change organisations, *Personnel Management*, Vol. 25, no. 1, pp. 32–5.

Beare, H., Caldwell, B. and Millikan, R. (1989) *Creating an Excellent School*, London: Routledge.

Belbin, M. (1981) *Management Teams: Why They Succeed or Fail*, London: Heinemann.

Belbin, M. (1993) *Team Roles at Work*, London: Butterworth-Heinemann.

Blanchard, K., Oncken, W. and Burrows, H. (1990) *The One Minute Manager Meets the Monkey*, London: Fontana/Collins.

Blanchard, K. and Peale, N. (1988) *The Power of Ethical Management*, London: Cedar.

Blunkett, D. (1997) Teaching: A Strong Profession, Speech by Secretary of State to North of England Conference, November.

Bolam, R., McMahan, A., Pocklington, K. and Weindling, D. (1993) *Effective Management in Schools*, London: HMSO.

Bolton, G. (1983) *Interviewing for Selection Decisions*, Windsor: NFER/Nelson.

Brain, G. (ed.) (1994) *Managing and Developing People*, Blagdon: The Staff College/Association for Colleges.

Buchan, J., Pearson, R. and Pike, G. (1988) Supply and demand for teachers in the 1990s, IMS Paper No. 151, Brighton: Institute of Manpower Studies.

Bush, T. (1994) Accountability in education, in Bush and West-Burnham *op. cit.*

Bush, T. (1995) Developing managers' training in institutes. Seminar for staff development in Polytechnics, Auckland, New Zealand.

Bush, T. (1995) *Theories of Educational Management*, second edition, London: Paul Chapman.

Bush, T. (1997a) The changing context of management in education, in Bush and Middlewood *op. cit.*

Bush, T. (1997b) Management Structures, in Bush and Middlewood, *op. cit.*

Bush, T. (1998) Organisational culture and strategic management, in Middlewood and Lumby, *op. cit.*

Bush, T. and Middlewood, D. (eds.) (1997) *Managing People in Education*, London: Paul Chapman.

Bush, T. and West-Burnham, J. (eds.) (1994) *The Principles of Educational Management*, Harlow: Longman.

Bush, T., Coleman, M., Wall, D. and West-Burnham, J. (1996) Mentoring and continuing professional development, in D. McIntyre and H. Haggar (eds.) *Mentors in Schools*, London: David Fulton.

Campbell, J. (1992) *Managing Teachers' Time in Primary Schools*, London: Trentham Books.

Campbell, J. and St J. Neill, R. (1997) Managing teachers' time under systemic reform, in Bush and Middlewood, *op. cit.*

Cardno, C. and Piggot-Irvine, E. (1997) *Effective Performance Appraisal*, Auckland, New Zealand: Addison Wesley Longman.

Cascio, W. (1991) *Applied Psychology in Personnel Management 4/e*, Englewood Cliffs, New Jersey: Prentice-Hall.

Chan, D. and Hui, E. (1995) Burnout and coping among Chinese secondary school teachers in Hong Kong, *British Journal of Educational Psychology*, Vol. 65, pp. 15–25.

Clay, J., Cole, M. and George, R. (1995) Visible minority ethnic representation in teaching and teacher education in Britain and the Netherlands: some observations, *Journal of Further and Higher Education*, Vol. 19, no. 2, Summer.

Cockburn, A. (1994) Teachers' experience of time: some implications for future research, *British Journal of Educational Studies*, Vol. 42, no. 4, pp. 375–87.

Coleman, M. (1995) *Women in Educational Management*, Distance Learning Materials for the Leicester University MBA, Leicester: Leicester University Press.

Coleman, M. (1994) Women in educational management, in Bush and West-Burnham, *op. cit.*

Coleman (1996) The management style of female headteachers, *Educational Management and Administration*, Vol. 24, no. 2, April.

Coleman, M. (1997) Managing induction and mentoring, in Bush and Middlewood, *op. cit.*

Coleman, M. and Bush, T. (1994) Managing with teams, in Bush and West-Burnham, *op. cit.*

Commission for Racial Equality (1988) *Ethnic Minority School Teachers: a Survey in Eight Local Education Authorities*, London: CRE.

Crawford, M. (1997) Managing stress, in Bush and Middlewood, *op. cit.*

Dalin, P. (1993) *Changing the School Culture*, London: Cassell.

Davidson, M. J. (1997) *The Black and Ethnic Minority Woman Manager: Cracking the Concrete Ceiling*, London: Paul Chapman.

Day, C. (1995) Leadership and professional development, in H. Busher and R. Saran (eds.) *Managing Teachers as Professionals in Schools*, London: Kogan Page.

Deal, T. (1985) The symbolism of effective schools, *Elementary School Journal*, pp. 85–95.

Deal, T. and Kennedy, A. (1982) *Corporate Cultures*, New York: Addison Wesley.

DES (1985) *Education for All: the Report of the Committee of Enquiry into the Education of Children from Ethnic Minority Groups*, the Swann Report, London: HMSO.

DES (1990) *Developing School Management: the Way Forward*, School Management Task Force, London: DES.

DfEE (1995) *Statistics of Education: Teachers England and Wales 1993*, London: HMSO.

Doring, A. (1993) Why me? Stress and the deputy, *British Journal of In-Service Education*, Vol. 19, no. 3, pp. 18–22.

Drucker, P. (1988) *Management*, London: Pan Books.

Drucker, P. F. (1989) The spirit of performance, in Riches and Morgan, *op. cit.*

Earley, P. (1993) Developing and using the standards, in D. Esp, *Competences for School Managers*, London: Kogan Page.

Earley, P. (1994) *Lecturers' Workload and Factors Affecting Stress Levels*, Windsor: NFER.

Earley, P. and Fletcher-Campbell, F. (1992) *Time to Manage? Department and Faculty Heads at Work*, Windsor: NFER/Nelson.

Earley, P. and Kinder, K. (1994) *Initial Rights: Effective Induction Practices for New Teachers*, Slough: NFER.

Ehrich, L. (1994) A mentoring programme for women educators, *School Organisation*, Vol. 14, no. 1, pp. 11–20.

Elliott, C. and Hall, V. (1994) F.E. inc – business orientation in further education and the introduction of HRM, *School Organisation*, Vol. 14, no. 1, pp. 3–10.

Elliott, G. (1996) *Crisis and Change in Vocational Education and Training*, London: Jessica Kingsley.

Esp, D. (1991) Staff development, local management of schools and governors, in L. Bell and C. Day (eds.) *Managing the Professional Development of Teachers*, Buckingham: Open University Press.

EU (1989) *European Framework Directive*. Council Directive 89/391/EEC.

Everard, B. and Morris, G. (1990) *Effective School Management*, second edition, London: Paul Chapman.

Fagg, V. (1991) Personnel management implications – pay and conditions of service. Workshop Session, Summer Conference, Central Hotel, Glasgow, The Association of Colleges for Further Education.

Fidler, B. (1988) Theory, concepts and experience in other organisations, in B. Fidler and R. Cooper (eds.) *Staff Appraisal in Schools and Colleges*, Harlow: Longman.

Fidler, B. (1993) Balancing the supply and demand for school teachers, in B. Fidler, B. Fugl and D. Esp (eds.) *The Supply and Recruitment of Teachers*, Harlow: Longman.

Fidler, B., Russell, S. and Simkins, T. (eds.) (1997) *Choices for Self-Managing Schools*, London: Paul Chapman.

Foreman, K. (1997) Managing individual performance, in Bush and Middlewood, *op. cit.*

Fowler, A. (1988) *Human Resource Management in Local Government*, Harlow: Longman.

Freeman, A. (1993) Women in education, *Educational Change and Development*, Vol. 13, no. 1, pp. 10–14.

Fullan, M. (1991) *The New Meaning of Educational Change*, London: Cassell.

Fullan, M. and Hargreaves, A. (1992) *What's Worth Fighting for in Your School*, Buckingham: Open University Press.

Galloway, D., Panckhurst, F., Boswell, K., Boswell, C. and Green, K. (1986) Sources of stress for primary school teachers in New Zealand, *British Educational Research Journal*, Vol. 12, no. 3, pp. 281–8.

Garratt, B. (1994) *The Learning Organisation*, revised edition, London: Harper Collins.

Gaziel, H. (1993) Coping with occupational stress among teachers: a cross-cultural study, *Comparative Education*, Vol. 29, no. 1, pp. 67–79.

Goss, D. (1994) *Principles of Human Resource Management*, London: Routledge.

Grace, G. (1995) *School Leadership: Beyond Education Management*, Lewes: Falmer Press.

Hackett, P. (1992) *Management: Personnel*, London: John Murray.

Hall, V. (1996) *Dancing on the Ceiling: A Study of Women Managers in Education*, London: Paul Chapman.

Hall, V. (1997a) Managing staff, in Fidler, Russell and Simkins, *op. cit.*

Hall, V. (1997b) Management roles in education, in Bush and Middlewood, *op. cit.*

Handy, C. (1993) *Understanding Organizations*, London: Penguin.

Handy, C. (1994) *The Empty Raincoat*, London: Hutchinson.

Handy, C. and Aitken, R. (1986) *Understanding Schools as Organisations*, Harmondsworth: Penguin Books.

Hargreaves, A. (1994) Postmodernity and the prospects for change, in A. Halsey, H. Lauder, P. Brown and A. Wells (eds.) *Education: Culture: Society*, Oxford: Oxford University Press.

Healy, G. and Calveley, M. (1998) Continuity and change in teachers' employment, *Employment Studies Paper 20*, Hertford: University of Hertforshire.

Healy, G. and Kraithman, D. (1994) An investigation into the impact of recent change on teachers' employment experience. Paper to the BUIRA Conference, Oxford.

Heasman, K. (1993) The case against ageism, *NATFE Journal*, Autumn, p. 28.

Herriott, P. (1989) *Recruitment in the Nineties*, London: Institute of Personnel Management.

Herzberg, F. (1966) *Work and the Nature of Man*, Cleveland, Ohio: World Publishing.

Hodgson, F. (1996) Appraisal trios – a case for The Three Musketeers, *Management in Education*, Vol. 10, no. 5, Winter, p. 33.

Hofstede, G. (1980) *Culture's Consequences*, Beverley Hills: Sage.

Holland, G. (1998) Into the twenty-first century, *New Childhood*, Vol. 13, no. 1, pp. 4–5.

Honey, P. (1991) The learning organisation simplified, *Training and Development*, July, pp. 30–3.

Hopkins, D., Ainscow, M. and West, M. (1994) *School Improvement in an Era of Change*, London: Cassell.

Hoyle, E. and Jones, K. (1995) *Professional Knowledge and Professional Practice*, London: Cassell.

Hoyle, E. and McCormick, R. (1976) *Innovation and the Teacher*, Milton Keynes: Open University Press.

Hume, C. (1990) *Effective Staff Selection in Schools*, Harlow: Longman.

Hunt, J. (1986) *Managing People at Work*, Maidenhead: McGraw-Hill.

Ironside, M. and Seifert, R. (1995) *Industrial Relations in Schools*, London: Routledge.

Jenkins, H. (1997) Leadership as cultural change, in Fidler, Russell and Simkins, *op. cit.*

Joiner, D. (1989) Assessment centres in the public sector, in Riches and Morgan, *op. cit.*

Jones, A. and Hendry, C. (1994) The learning organization: adult learning and organizational transformation, *British Journal of Management*, Vol. 5, pp. 153–62.

Jones, J. and Mathias, J. (1995) *Training for Appraisal and Professional Development*, London: Cassell.

Joyce, B. and Showers, B. (1980) Improving inservice training: the messages of research, *Educational Leadership*, Vol. 37, pp. 379–86.

Jurasinghe, D. and Lyons, G. (1996) *The Competent Head*, Lewes: Falmer Press.

Kakabadse, A. (1983) *The Politics of Management*, Aldershot: Gower Press.

Kakabadse, A., Ludlow, R. and Vinnicombe, S. (1987) *Working in Organisations*, Aldershot: Gower Press.

Katzenbach, J. and Smith, D. (1993) *The Wisdom of Teams*, New York: Harper Business.

Kelly, M. (1995) Action first – thinking later! *Management in Education*, Vol. 9, no. 2, April, pp. 10–12.

Kinder, K., Harland, J. and Wootten, M. (1991) *The Impact of School Focused Inset on Classroom Practice*, Slough: NFER.

Kremer-Hayon, L. and Goldstein, Z. (1990) The inner world of Israeli secondary school teachers: work centrality, job satisfaction and stress, *Comparative Education*, Vol. 26, pp. 285–9.

Kyriacou, C. (1987) Teacher stress and burnout: an international review, *Educational Research*, Vol. 29, no. 2, June, pp. 146–52.

Leithwood, K. (1996) Doing business in restructuring schools: what is team learning anyway? *1996 Yearbook of Management and Administration*, National Association of Professors of Educational Administration.

Levacic, R. (1997) Managing resources in educational institutions: an open systems approach, in M. Preedy, R. Glatter and R. Levacic (eds.) *Educational Management: Strategy, Quality and Resources*, Buckingham: Open University Press.

Liddle, J. and Joshi, R. (1987) Class and gender among professional women in India, in A. Spencer and D. Podmore (eds.) *In a Man's World: Essays on Women in Male-Dominated Professions*, London: Tavistock.

Little, J. (1990) Teachers as colleagues, in A. Lieberman (ed.) *Schools as Collaborative Cultures*, Lewes: Falmer Press.

Lumby, J. (1997) The Learning Organization, in T. Bush and D. Middlewood (eds.) *op. cit.*

MacFarlane, J. (1998) When old uncertainties disappear, *Times Educational Supplement*, 30 January.

Maier, F. (1976) *The Appraisal Interview: Three Basic Approaches*, La Jolla, California: University Associates Inc.

Marshall, C. (1994) Introduction, in C. Marshall (ed.) *The New Politics of Race and Gender*, London: Falmer Press.

Maslow, A. (1943) A theory of human motivation, *Psychological Review*, Vol. 50, pp. 370–96.

McClelland, D. (1961) *The Achieving Society*, Princeton: Van Nostrand.

McGregor, D. (1970) *The Human Side of Enterprise*, Maidenhead: McGraw-Hill.

Megginson, D. and Clutterbuck, D. (1997) *Mentoring in Action*, London: Kogan Page.

Middlewood, D. (1994) Distinction between mentor and line manager, in J. O'Neill, D. Middlewood and D. Glover, *Managing Human Resources in Schools and Colleges*, Harlow: Longman.

Middlewood, D., Blount, J., Sharman, M. and Fay, C. (1995) *Evaluation of Teacher Appraisal in Northamptonshire*, Northampton: Northamptonshire County Council.

Middlewood, D. (1997a) Managing appraisal, in Bush and Middlewood, *op. cit.*

Middlewood, D. (1997b) Managing recruitment and selection, in Bush and Middlewood, *op. cit.*

Middlewood, D. (1997c) Managing staff development, in Bush and Middlewood, *op. cit.*

Middlewood, D. (1998) Strategic management in education: an overview, in Middlewood and Lumby, *op. cit.*

Middlewood, D. and Lumby, J. (eds.) (1998) *Strategic Management in Schools and Colleges*, London: Paul Chapman.

Middlewood, D. and Parker, R. (1998) Staff Development for School Improvement, in *Professional Development Today*, Vol. 1, issue 3.

Montgomery, D. and Hadfield, N. (1989) *Practical Teacher Appraisal*, London: Kogan Page.

Morgan, C. (1989) Inside the interview black box, in Riches and Morgan, *op. cit.*

Morgan, C. (1997) Selection: predicting effective performance, in L. Kydd, M. Crawford and C. Riches (eds.) *Professional Development for Educational Management*, Buckingham: Open University Press.

Morgan, C., Hall, V. and Mackay, H. (1985) *The Selection of Secondary Head Teachers*, Milton Keynes: Open University Press.

Morgan, G. (1996) *Images of Organisation*, London: Sage Publications.

Mortimore, P., Mortimore, J. with Thomas, H. (1994) *Managing Associate Staff*, London: Paul Chapman.

Mullins, L. (1989) *Management and Organisational Behaviour*, second edition, London: Pitman.

Mwamwenda, T. S. (1995) Job satisfaction among secondary school teachers in Transkei, *South African Journal of Education*, Vol. 15, no. 2, pp. 84–7.

NCE (1993a) *Learning to Succeed*, London: Heinemann.

NCE (1993b) *Against the Odds*, London: Heinemann.

Nias, J., Southworth, G. and Yeomans, R. (1989) *Staff Relationships in the Primary School*, London: Cassell.

Ofsted (1995) *A Framework for the Inspection of Schools*, London: HMSO.

Ofsted and Audit Commission (1993) *Unfinished Business*, London: HMSO.

Oldroyd, D. and Hall, V. (1991) *Managing Staff Development: a Handbook for Secondary Schools*, London: Paul Chapman.

O'Neill, J. (1994a) Managing human resources, in Bush and West-Burnham, *op. cit.*

O'Neill, J. (1994b) *Managing Through Teams in Schools and Colleges*, Leicester: University of Leicester.

O'Neill, J. (1997) Managing through teams, in Bush and Middlewood, *op. cit.*

Osler, A. (1997) *The Education and Careers of Black Teachers*, Buckingham: Open University Press.

Ouston, J. (1993) Management competences, school effectiveness and educational management, *Management & Administration*, Vol. 21, no. 4, pp. 212–21.

Paisey, A. (ed.) (1985) *Jobs in Schools: Applying, Interviewing and Selecting for Appointments and Promotions*, London: Heinemann.

Peters, T. (1989) *Thriving on Chaos*, London: Pan/Macmillan.

Peters, T. and Waterman, R. (1982) *In Search of Excellence*, New York: Harper Collins.

Pierce, M. and Molloy, G. (1990) Psychological and biographical differences between secondary school teachers experiencing high and low levels of burnout, *British Journal of Educational Psychology*, Vol. 60, pp. 37–51.

Plant, R. (1987) *Managing Change and Making it Stick*, London: Fontana Press.

Poster, C. and Poster, D. (1993) The nature of appraisal, in L. Kydd, M. Crawford and C. Riches (eds.) *Professional Development for Educational Management*, Buckingham: Open University Press.

Punch, K. and Tuettmann, E. (1990) Correlates of psychological distress among secondary school teachers, *British Educational Research Journal*, Vol. 16, no. 4, pp. 369–82.

Rees, F. (1989) *Teacher Stress: an Exploratory Study*, London: NFER.

Riches, C. (1983) The interview in education, in O. Boyd-Barrett, T. Bush, J. Goody, I. McNay and M. Preedy (eds.) *Approaches to Post School Management*, London: Harper & Row.

Riches, C. (1994a) Motivation, in Bush and West-Burnham, *op. cit.*

Riches, C. (1994b) Communication, in Bush and West-Burnham, *op. cit.*

Riches, C. (1997) Managing for people and performance, in Bush and Middlewood, *op. cit.*

Riches, C. and Morgan, C. (1989) *Human Resource Management in Education*, Milton Keynes: Open University Press.

Ronan, W. and Prien, E. (1971) *Perspectives on the Measurement of Human Performance*, New York: Appleton-Century-Crofts.

Rujis, A. (1993) Women managers in education: a worldwide progress report, *Coombe Lodge Report*, Vol. 23, no. 7/8.

Sammons, P., Hillman, J. and Mortimore, P. (1995) *Key Characteristics of Effective Schools: a Review of School Effectiveness*, London: Ofsted.

Sammons, P., Thomas, S. and Mortimore, P. (1997) *Forging Links: Effective Schools and Effective Departments*, London: Paul Chapman.

Saran, R. and Busher, H. (1995) Working with support staff in schools: relationships between teachers, governors and other staff, in H. Busher and R. Saran (eds.) *Managing Teachers as Professionals in Schools*, London: Kogan Page.

Schagen, I. and Morrison, J. (1997) *Quase: Quantitative Analysis for Self-Evaluation*, Slough: NFER.

Schein, E. (1978) *Career Dynamics*, New York: Addison Wesley.

Scott, W. (1987) *Organisations: Rational, Natural and Open Systems*, second edition, Englewood Cliffs, New Jersey: Prentice-Hall.

Select Committee on Education and Employment (1998) *Report on the Supply and Recruitment of Qualified Teachers in England and Wales 1993–96*, London: HMSO.

Senge, P. (1990) *The Fifth Discipline*, London: Doubleday.

Sergiovanni, T. (1984) Cultural and competing perspectives in administrative theory and practice, in T. Sergiovanni and J. Corbally (eds.) *Leadership and Organisational Culture*, Chicago: University of Illinois Press.

Sinclair, A. (1992) The tyranny of a team ideology, *Organisation Studies*, Vol. 12, no. 14, pp. 611–26.

Sivasubramanian, N. and Ratnam, C. (1998) The relationship between human resource management and firm performance, *Paradigm*, Vol. 1, no. 2, pp. 135–41.

Smith, P. (1993) Overview and introduction, in P. Smith and J. West-Burnham (eds.) *Mentoring in the Effective School*, Harlow: Longman.

Southworth, G. (1990) *Staff Selection in the Primary School*, Oxford: Blackwell.

Southworth, G. (1994) The learning school, in R. Ribbins and E. Burridge (eds.) *Improving Education: Promoting Quality in Schools*, London: Cassell.

Squire, W. (1989) The aetiology of a defective theory, in Riches and Morgan, *op. cit.*

Stoll, L. and Fink, D. (1998) The cruising school, in L. Stoll and K. Myers (eds.) *No Quick Fixes: Perspectives on Schools in Difficulty*, London: Falmer Press.

Taylor, F. and Hemmingway, J. (1990) *Picking the Team*, Video Arts for DES.

Thomson, R. (1993) *Managing People*, Oxford: Butterworth-Heineman.

Times Educational Supplement (1993) Heads check the fish, TES, 20 May, London: Times Newspapers.

Travers, C. and Cooper, C. (1996) *Teachers Under Pressure*, London: Cassell.

Tuckman, B. (1965) Developmental sequences in small groups, *Psychological Bulletin*, Vol. 63, pp. 384–99.

Turner, C. (1992) *Motivating Staff*, Mendip Paper 033, Blagdon: the Staff College.

Vaarlem, A., Nuttall, D. and Walker, A. (1992) *What Makes Teachers Tick? A Survey of Teacher Morale and Motivation*, London: Centre for Educational Research.

Vandevelde, B. R. (1988) *Implications of Motivation Theories and Work Motivation Studies for the Redeployment of Teachers*, Sheffield: Sheffield City Polytechnic Centre for Education Management and Administration.

Van Velzen, W. and Robin, D. (1985) *The Need for School Improvement in the Next Decade*, Antwerp: Acco Publishers.

Vosper, K. and Smith, P. (1993) Recognising lesbian and gay rights, *NATFE Journal*, Autumn, p. 28.

Wagstaff, J. (1994) HRM in the next decade – an external perspective, in G. Brain (ed.) *Managing and Developing People*, Blagdon: The Staff College.

Wallace, M. and Hall, V. (1994) *Inside the SMT: Teamwork in Secondary School Management*, London: Paul Chapman.

Warner, D. and Crosthwaite, E. (1993) People are the first priority, *Education*, Vol. 180, no. 7, pp. 128–9.

Werner, W. (1991) Defining curriculum policy through slogans, *Journal of Curriculum Policy*, Vol. 6, no. 2, pp. 225–38.

West, P. (1994) The concept of the learning organisation, *Journal of European Industrial Training*, Vol. 18, no. 1, pp. 15–21.

West-Burnham, J. (1992) *Managing Quality in Schools*, second edition, Harlow: Longman.

Whittington, R. (1993) *What is Strategy and Does it Matter?* London: Routledge.

Wragg, E., Wikeley, F., Wragg, C. and Haynes, G. (1996) *Teacher Appraisal Observed*, London: Routledge.

Author Index

N.C.I LIBRARY

Subject Index